The Power of Words

Psychological Strategies for Effective Communication

By
Jonathan S. Hale

The Power of Words

Psychological Strategies for Effective Communication

Table of Contents

Introduction

In an era where connection defines success and fulfillment, the art of communication stands as a pillar of our daily lives. Whether it's building lasting relationships, advancing in our careers, or simply expressing our thoughts, the ability to communicate effectively is paramount. Yet, what often appears as a simple exchange of words is layered with psychological intricacies that govern how we perceive, interpret, and respond to each other. This book aims to unravel these complexities by providing readers with psychological strategies designed to enhance communication skills, influence others, and build meaningful connections.

Communication is, at its core, a profound exchange that goes beyond verbal articulation. It's a dance of ideas, emotions, and intentions, meticulously woven through words, gestures, and shared silences. The nuances of communication are shaped by our thoughts, experiences, and the subconscious cues we often overlook. The journey toward mastering this art begins with understanding the psychology underpinning our interactions. From the foundations of effective communication to the advanced techniques of persuasion, this book serves as a comprehensive guide to navigating the multifaceted world of human connection.

Our exploration begins by laying the groundwork with an understanding of how psychological principles shape the way we communicate. This foundational knowledge sets the stage for a deeper dive into specific aspects of communication, including perception, nonverbal cues, and active listening. Each element contributes a crucial piece to the puzzle, allowing us to craft messages that resonate and build rapport with others. By honing these skills, we enhance our ability to reach others on a profound level, fostering genuine connections that are both impactful and enduring.

The power of perception cannot be understated. It shapes not only our interactions but also our interpretations of them. Misperceptions can lead to misunderstandings, while clarity of perception paves the way for conversations that connect and inspire. Understanding how perception works and learning to overcome misperceptions opens doors to more meaningful dialogue and fewer communication barriers. This knowledge is pivotal, especially in a world brimming with diverse perspectives and cultural influences.

Nonverbal communication, too, plays a critical role. Our bodies often speak louder than words, transmitting feelings and attitudes before we even utter a syllable. From subtle gestures to facial expressions and body language, our nonverbal cues are powerful communicators of intent and emotion. Learning to read these cues and being mindful of our own enhances our ability to interact effectively and empathetically.

Active listening is another vital component of effective communication. In a fast-paced world where everyone seems eager to speak, the value of listening is often overshadowed. Yet, genuine listening fosters understanding and connection. By employing techniques to improve our listening skills and overcoming barriers that hinder our attention, we become better communicators—able to engage in dialogues that are not only productive but deeply enriching.

Moreover, how we craft our messages significantly impacts their reception. Word choice and message structure can make or break the effectiveness of our communication. Whether it's a casual conversation or a formal presentation, the ability to articulate thoughts with clarity and precision is a hallmark of impactful communication. This book provides insights into tailoring one's message for maximum effect, ensuring that the intended message is the one that's received.

Beyond individual interactions, the principles of communication extend to group dynamics and professional settings. Effective team interaction, resolving conflicts, and building leadership capabilities are all rooted in communication prowess. By exploring these themes, we can better navigate the intricacies of workplace dynamics and harness the power of communication to lead and influence effectively.

At the heart of this book is the belief that communication is a pathway to personal development and transformation. As we refine our communication skills, we not only improve our ability to connect with others but also deepen our understanding of ourselves. The journey through these chapters promises to equip readers with the tools needed to communicate with confidence, empathy, and integrity in every facet of life.

Communication is not just about exchanging information; it's about understanding the emotions and intentions behind the information. As we delve deeper, we explore advanced concepts like emotional intelligence and the ethical side of communication. These components emphasize the importance of being not only articulate but also empathetic and principled in our interactions.

In these pages, you'll find a synthesis of research, practical examples, and actionable strategies, all aimed at enhancing your communication skills. The interplay of theory and application provides a balanced approach that transforms knowledge into skill. This evolution from understanding to mastery prepares you for diverse scenarios, whether it's a challenging conversation, a cross-cultural interaction, or leveraging the latest digital platforms for effective communication.

Ultimately, the goal is growth—both personal and relational. As we unwrap the potential of communication, we uncover pathways to strengthen resilience, cultivate empathy, and inspire others. These outcomes are not merely aspirational but achievable, rooted in the practical tools and insights offered throughout this journey.

We invite you to embark on this journey of discovery and mastery in communication. Through understanding, practice, and reflection, you can unlock the power within you to communicate with purpose, influence, and authenticity. Whether you're seeking to improve personal relationships or to assert leadership across various landscapes, this book is your companion, guiding you toward a more connected, impactful, and fulfilling life.

Chapter 1: Understanding the Psychology of Communication

In the realm of human interaction, understanding the psychology of communication reveals profound insights that can unlock the potential within every exchange. At its core, communication is an intricate dance of words, emotions, and intentions, where the mind's cognitive processes play a leading role. This chapter delves into the foundational elements that make communication effective, exploring key psychological principles that govern how we convey thoughts and feelings. By examining the subconscious drivers behind our words, we can harness the power to connect deeply and authentically with others. The art of persuasion, the science of empathy, and the dynamics of human behavior all intertwine to create a tapestry of understanding and resonance. This is not merely about transferring information but about crafting memorable interactions that influence and inspire. With the right tools and mindset, anyone can elevate their ability to engage meaningfully, paving the way for stronger relationships and impactful dialogues.

The Foundations of Effective Communication

Communication is at the heart of human interaction, shaping our relationships and influencing how we connect with each other. To communicate effectively, it's crucial to understand the underlying psychological frameworks that guide our exchange of ideas and emotions. At its core, effective communication is about more than just the words we say; it encompasses a deep understanding of emotional dynamics, intention, and interpretation.

The foundation of effective communication begins with self-awareness. Awareness of one's own emotions, biases, and intentions is the first step in creating meaningful dialogue. When we're aware of our reactions and the subconscious cues we project, we're better equipped to manage our interactions constructively. By understanding ourselves, we gain the ability to present our thoughts with clarity and sincerity, reducing the likelihood of misunderstandings.

Equally essential is the ability to empathize with others. Empathy serves as a bridge that allows us to step into another person's shoes and view the world from their perspective. This emotional intelligence not only facilitates more profound connections but also ensures that our responses are considerate and respectful. When we communicate with empathy, we validate the experiences and emotions of others, fostering a sense of trust and rapport.

In conversations, clarity and intention form the bedrock of effective communication. Without a clear purpose or intention, messages can easily become muddled. Setting an intention helps in focusing the conversation, ensuring that the key points are understood and the objectives are clear. Clarity in communication doesn't mean oversimplifying the message; rather, it involves articulating thoughts in a manner that minimizes confusion and maximizes understanding.

Active listening is another fundamental component. It's not enough to merely hear the words being spoken; active listening involves fully engaging with the speaker, showing genuine interest, and providing feedback. This commitment to listening encourages speakers to open up, thus enhancing the depth and quality of the conversation. As we attune our listening skills, we become better communicators—able to respond appropriately and enrich the dialogue.

Nonverbal communication also plays a pivotal role. Our body language, facial expressions, and even our posture convey messages that are often more impactful than speech. Nonverbal cues can affirm or contradict the spoken word, subsequently influencing the interpretation and reaction of others. Mastering the art of nonverbal communication ensures that every aspect of our message aligns harmoniously.

To build a strong foundation in communication, investing in building rapport cannot be overlooked. Rapport creates a resonance between individuals, one that is characterized by mutual understanding and respect. This bond makes communication more effective because it reduces resistance and enhances the willingness to share openly. Establishing rapport doesn't happen overnight—it requires patience, authenticity, and a consistent effort to engage with others meaningfully.

Language choice also has a significant impact. The words we choose and how we structure our statements can strongly influence the outcome of our interactions. Thoughtful language not only expresses respect but also reflects an awareness of the impact words have on others. Moreover, crafting messages that are relatable and persuasive can turn even the most challenging conversations into opportunities for positive outcomes.

In the digital age, communication extends beyond face-to-face interactions. The ability to adapt these foundational principles to various communication platforms—whether over email, social media, or virtual meetings—is increasingly important. While technology offers vast opportunities for connectivity, it requires us to be even more mindful of how we convey tone and emotion through text.

Building and maintaining these foundations takes practice and dedication. By committing to these principles, individuals can transform their communication from a mere exchange of information to a powerful tool for connection and influence. As we navigate complex interpersonal dynamics, these foundational skills become invaluable, allowing us to inspire and make lasting impacts on those around us.

Strengthening your communication skills is not just about improving interactions in professional settings; it's also about enhancing personal relationships. Whether it's navigating family discussions, negotiating with peers, or simply engaging in meaningful conversations with friends, the principles of effective communication remain steadfastly applicable. By embracing these foundations, anyone can achieve better understanding and connection in all areas of life.

Key Psychological Principles

The art of communication is grounded in a myriad of psychological principles that govern how we interact, influence, and understand one another. These principles form the bedrock of effective communication by offering insights into human behavior and thought processes. One fundamental psychological principle is the notion of perception, which shapes how messages are received and interpreted. How we perceive others and the world around us directly influences our communication style. This perceptual lens can vary greatly from one individual to another, affecting everything from word choice to emotional responses.

An essential principle to consider is the role of attention in communication. Attention dictates where cognitive resources are allocated during an interaction. By understanding what captures or diverts attention, communicators can better structure their messages to hold interest and convey crucial information. This awareness helps in making conversations more engaging and memorable, allowing communicators to drive their messages home with impact.

In understanding these dynamics, we must also explore the concept of cognitive biases, which are systemic patterns of deviation from norm or rationality in judgment. These biases affect how people interpret information and make decisions. For example, the confirmation bias leads individuals to favor information that confirms their existing beliefs, dismissing contrary data. Recognizing this can aid communicators in crafting messages that resonate more deeply by aligning with the audience's inherent inclinations.

Emotions play a pivotal role in communication, intertwining with psychological principles to color interactions. Emotional intelligence, or the ability to perceive, control, and evaluate emotions, is crucial for effective communication. It involves recognizing one's own emotions and those of others to foster a connection and engagement. Emotional cues guide communicators in tailoring their messages to the emotional states of their audience, which is key in persuading and influencing effectively.

Another key principle is the social context in which communication occurs. The environment and social norms dictate what is appropriate or expected in any given interaction. Awareness of social context includes understanding cultural nuances and the implicit rules that govern communication within different groups. This knowledge enables communicators to navigate diverse interactions with sensitivity, ensuring that messages are both effective and respectful.

Additionally, the principle of reciprocal altruism is woven into the fabric of communication. This psychological principle suggests that individuals are motivated to help others with the expectation of future reciprocation. In communication, this can manifest as sharing information, offering support, or engaging in cooperative dialogues. Understanding this principle can help communicators build rapport and trust, fostering long-term relationships and collaborative environments.

The dynamics of power and influence also play a significant role in communication. Power, in a communicative sense, involves the ability to affect others' thoughts, emotions, or actions. Understanding the power dynamics between communicators allows for a more strategic approach in persuasion and negotiation. Messages can be crafted to minimize resistance and build consensus, taking into account the perceived power relationship between participants.

Certain psychological principles relate to message framing and timing. The framing of a message — how it is structured and presented — significantly affects its persuasiveness. A well-framed message can underscore positive outcomes or alleviate perceived risks, guiding the audience towards a desired viewpoint. Similarly, timing is critical; delivering a message at the right moment can enhance its impact, while poor timing can undermine even the most carefully crafted communications.

Language and linguistics also play into key psychological principles of communication. The choice of words, tone, and syntax all contribute to how messages are perceived. For example, using inclusive language fosters a sense of belonging and collaboration. Understanding the subtleties of verbal communication can empower individuals to express themselves more clearly and to better connect with their audience.

Feedback loops are another vital principle in communication psychology. They involve the continuous process of exchanging information and adjusting messages based on feedback received. Effective communicators leverage feedback to refine their approach, ensuring alignment with audience needs and expectations. This adaptability is crucial in dynamic and ever-shifting communicative contexts.

Memory retention and recall also play into psychological principles that affect communication. Communicators who understand how memory works can structure messages in ways that enhance retention and recall. Techniques like repetition, storytelling, and association help anchor information, making it more accessible when needed. By tapping into these mechanisms, communicators can ensure that their messages have a lasting impact.

In sum, understanding these key psychological principles equips individuals with the tools to communicate more effectively. It allows for the crafting of messages that are not only clear and persuasive but also grounded in an empathetic understanding of human nature. By embracing these principles, communicators can transcend superficial interactions and forge meaningful, lasting connections.

Chapter 2: The Role of Perception in Communication

Perception plays a pivotal role in how we communicate, shaping the very fabric of our interactions and influencing the impact of our messages. It's like wearing a pair of tinted glasses; everything we see—every word we hear—is colored by our personal experiences, beliefs, and biases. This subjective view can enhance mutual understanding when aligned with others, or it can create barriers when misaligned, leading to misinterpretations and conflicts. Recognizing this, we hold the power to refine our perceptual filters, actively seeking clarity and empathy in our exchanges. By consciously adjusting how we perceive others, and simultaneously becoming aware of how they might perceive us, we unlock the potential to foster authentic connections. It's this undercurrent of awareness that elevates ordinary dialogue to a level where real understanding, influence, and trust can flourish, proving that perception is not just a passive reception but an active component in the art of communication.

How Perception Shapes Conversations

In the intricate dance of communication, perception acts as a silent partner, guiding and shaping the flow of dialogue without uttering a single word. Our perception - the lens through which we see and interpret the world - influences every exchange we have. It's like the glasses we wear that shade everything we perceive, influenced by past experiences, beliefs, and emotions. Just think about a time when you interpreted a friend's comment as criticism when they meant it as a joke. Such are the misunderstandings born of perception.

We don't always realize how deeply our perceptions impact our interactions. As we walk into a conversation, we carry with us our interpretations of the other person's words and actions. These perceptions are not just passively received; they are actively constructed from what we believe about ourselves and others. This construction affects the way we respond, shaping the dialogue's outcome long before a word is spoken.

Consider the role of expectations. When you expect positive interactions, you tend to listen with an open mind, seek understanding, and respond with empathy. But if you carry a chip on your shoulder, worried others will dismiss your ideas, you might misinterpret friendly remarks as hostile critiques. It's a self-fulfilling prophecy where perception doesn't just reflect reality – it creates it.

So, how can we use this knowledge to improve our conversations? Awareness is the key. Recognizing that what we see might not be what's truly there helps us pause and question our initial judgments. It's about turning that automatic perception switch off and stepping back to ask ourselves, "Is this what really happened? Or is this just my interpretation?"

Take, for instance, the act of paraphrasing. By articulating back what you've heard, you verify your understanding of the other person's message. This simple technique doesn't just clear up potential misperceptions; it also demonstrates that you're actively engaged in trying to understand. Such transparency in communication paves the way for richer, more productive conversations.

Empathy also plays a crucial role in reshaping perceptions. By putting ourselves in others' shoes, we can start to see how they might perceive the world differently from us. This doesn't mean abandoning our views but enriching them with a broader perspective. It's like viewing a painting from different angles; each angle adds depth and understanding to the artwork.

Furthermore, the narratives we construct about the people we're interacting with can alter the course of the dialogue. When we think of someone as an ally rather than an adversary, we're more likely to approach interactions with openness and curiosity. This positive framing encourages cooperation and mutual respect, transforming potential conflicts into collaborative opportunities.

In professional settings, an awareness of perception is vital. For example, leaders who understand how their team perceives them can better tailor their communication to inspire and motivate. An employee who perceives their manager as supportive is more likely to offer innovative ideas without fear of judgment. Here, perception becomes a powerful tool to foster a thriving work environment.

Similarly, perception plays a crucial role in cross-cultural communication. Cultural backgrounds shape how people interpret words, gestures, and even silence. What might be seen as politeness in one culture could be perceived as evasiveness in another. By being conscious of these differences and striving to understand them, we can bridge cultural gaps and create more harmonious interactions.

It's also important to consider how technology influences our perception in conversations. Text messages and emails strip away the nuances of tone and body language, often leading to misinterpretations. In the absence of these cues, our perceptions fill in the blanks, sometimes inaccurately. Selecting the right medium for each interaction can aid in conveying messages more accurately and can impact how our perceptions are formed.

Understanding perception as an active participant in our conversations leads us to improved communication strategies. By remaining conscious of the lenses through which we view interactions, engaging empathetically with others, and choosing appropriate communication methods, we take control of the narrative, steering dialogues toward more positive outcomes. This mindful approach not only enriches our personal conversations but also enhances our professional and cross-cultural interactions, making the tapestry of our communicative life more intricate and profound.

Overcoming Misperceptions

Perception, often colored by past experiences, biases, and emotions, acts as a filter through which we interpret and understand the world around us. In communication, this filter can give rise to misperceptions, leading to misunderstandings and conflict. Overcoming these misperceptions is key to enhancing our communication skills, fostering deeper connections, and ensuring our messages are accurately conveyed.

Imagine walking into a room where a heated debate is taking place. The words exchanged are just a part of what you'd perceive; their tone, body language, and even the silence can be equally revealing, yet potentially misleading. Our brains are wired to fill in gaps based on subtle cues, but sometimes they get it wrong. The trick lies in recognizing and adjusting for these errors. Successful communicators excel by honing the ability to identify and address potential areas of misperception before they escalate.

To get started, we need to acknowledge our biases. Every single one of us interprets conversations through the lens of our personal history. For example, two people hearing the same phrase might walk away with entirely different understandings because of differing backgrounds and expectations. Accepting that our perspective might not always be the complete truth is a powerful step towards combating misperceptions. It fosters an openness that allows for inquiry, dialogue, and ultimately, a more profound understanding.

Active listening plays a pivotal role in navigating and correcting misperceptions. It involves more than just hearing words; it requires engaging with the speaker's intent and underlying emotions. By reflecting on what the other person has said, summarizing their points, and asking clarifying questions, we engage in a process that enhances understanding on both ends. This practice discourages assumptions, which often fuel misperceptions, and encourages a focus on what is actually being communicated rather than what one might expect or fear to hear.

Moreover, the art of rephrasing or paraphrasing can serve as an effective tool in overcoming misperceptions. By expressing what we understand in our own words and seeking confirmation, we not only clarify our interpretation but also demonstrate empathy and respect for the speaker's perspective. This creates a space for correcting misunderstandings and building mutual trust.

Nonverbal communication channels also contribute significantly to perceptions and misperceptions. A simple frown or crossed arms can be interpreted as disapproval or discomfort, even when none was intended. By expanding our knowledge and awareness of body language, we can better interpret these signals and avoid jumping to conclusions. Similarly, being mindful of our own nonverbal cues helps ensure we're not unintentionally sending mixed messages.

Empathy acts as a bridge over the chasms created by misperceptions. When we strive to see the world from another's viewpoint, we limit the room for misunderstanding. By asking ourselves, "How might they be feeling?" or "Why might they respond this way?", we start seeing communication as a shared experience rather than a one-sided transaction. Empathy encourages patience and understanding, qualities that mitigate the risks of forming inaccurate interpretations.

Another effective strategy is adjusting your communication style to suit your audience. By tailoring our language, tone, and approach to the needs and expectations of others, we minimize the potential for misinterpretation. This requires a certain level of self-awareness and adaptability but is crucial for achieving clarity and connection.

Acknowledging the power of feedback is also critical when working to overcome misperceptions. Constructive feedback from others can illuminate blind spots and offer alternative viewpoints that widen our understanding. By actively seeking such input, we engage in a continuous learning process, refining our communication skills over time.

Of course, overcoming misperceptions isn't just about understanding others better—it also involves managing how we're perceived. This dual approach, where we fine-tune both our interpretations and our conveyance, maximizes communicative efficiency and efficacy. By striving for clarity in our expressions and nurturing a receptive attitude towards responses, we create an environment where dialogue can flourish without the encumbrance of misunderstandings.

Ultimately, in our journey to master effective communication, the ability to overcome misperceptions is indispensable. It requires a commitment to learning, growth, and the willingness to remain open and flexible in the face of complexity. Through these efforts, we not only enhance our direct conversations but foster a larger culture of understanding and positivity, crucial elements for thriving personal and professional relationships.

Chapter 3: The Power of Nonverbal Communication

Nonverbal communication, those subtle signals and cues, wields an undeniable influence in our interactions, often speaking louder than words themselves. An unspoken language composed of gestures, facial expressions, posture, and even the space we maintain, these elements can shape perceptions, build connections, or sow misunderstandings without a single word uttered. It's in the arch of an eyebrow, the crossing of arms, or the distance we keep that others find insight into our true feelings and intentions, sometimes before we've even spoken. To master this silent symphony is to harness a profound power, one that can enhance relationships, make presentations unforgettable, and disarm potential conflicts before they escalate. By becoming more attuned to these silent conversations, we sharpen our ability to respond effectively, building bridges with empathy and authenticity. As we delve into the potential of nonverbal communication, remember that it's not just about interpreting others; it's equally about being aware of the messages we unknowingly convey in every interaction.

The Influence of Body Language

Nonverbal communication is a craft that's long been underestimated in its power to influence. Body language comprises a broad range of physical cues, from subtle to overt, that can dramatically shape the outcome of interactions. Whether you're giving a presentation, negotiating, or simply engaging in a casual conversation, your body speaks volumes before you utter a word. Understanding these physical cues and learning to control them can be transformative in enhancing communication effectiveness.

One of the most fascinating aspects of body language is its universality. Across cultures, certain gestures and expressions have similar meanings. A smile, for instance, is generally recognized as a sign of friendliness or approval. Yet, nuances exist, and context plays a critical role. To influence others successfully, it's crucial you recognize both the universal signs and cultural variations. This awareness not only helps in conveying your intended message but also in reading others accurately.

Our facial expressions, for instance, are incredibly rich in information. The micro-expressions that flash across our faces can betray our genuine emotions, despite attempts to conceal them. Mastering the ability to read these brief signals can give you insights into the thoughts and feelings of those you're communicating with, allowing you to respond with greater empathy and understanding.

Moreover, gestures enhance the clarity and impact of your speech. Dynamic hand movements can underscore enthusiasm and conviction, making your communication more engaging. However, it's essential to balance this with context and audience expectations. Overusing gestures can come off as aggressive or overwhelming, while underuse can make interactions dull.

Posture is another key component of body language that significantly influences how your message is perceived. An open stance suggests approachability and confidence, while crossed arms may be seen as defensive or closed off. Being mindful of your stance can help in presenting yourself as receptive and engaged, encouraging more open communication in return.

Certain body language elements serve as indicators of confidence, which is pivotal in persuasive communication. Eye contact, for instance, demonstrates confidence and interest. However, the fine line between confident eye contact and an intimidating gaze must be tread carefully. Frequent shifts in eye contact are perceived as shifty, while steady, yet natural eye contact builds trust and respect.

Beyond facial expressions and gestures, proxemics—the use of space in communication—plays a crucial role. By respecting personal space, you're more likely to make the person feel comfortable and valued. Conversely, encroaching upon someone's personal space can lead to discomfort and defensiveness. Understanding and adapting to these spatial signals can enhance mutual respect and facilitate smoother exchanges.

Touch is another powerful nonverbal cue. Appropriate use of touch, such as a handshake or a supportive pat on the back, can reinforce messages of camaraderie and support. Yet, this is one area where cultural sensitivities are particularly pronounced. Each context and relationship demands a thoughtful approach to employing touch authentically and respectfully.

Voice tone, while often categorized alongside verbal communication, leans heavily into nonverbal terrain when it comes to influencing others. The same words spoken in a soft, calm voice can convey warmth, whereas a high-pitched tone may suggest anxiety or excitement. Modulating your voice to match the message you aim to deliver is an art that, when mastered, elevates your communicative ability substantially.

The intricate relationship between verbal and nonverbal cues cannot be overstated. Verbal communication backed by congruent body language amplifies the message and builds persuasive power. However, when there's a mismatch between words and actions, people tend to trust actions over words. This is why politicians, leaders, and managers spend significant time perfecting their body language, ensuring it aligns with their spoken messages to project authenticity and trustworthiness.

Effective body language isn't about manipulation; it's about embodying authenticity. This authenticity in your gestures, posture, and facial expressions fosters genuine connections. When others perceive your nonverbal cues as sincere, it invites openness and trust, which are essential for influencing and forging strong relationships.

Practicing mindfulness in noticing and understanding the nonverbal signals of those around you enriches your ability to tailor your communication. This attunement nurtures greater emotional intelligence and empathy, allowing for healthier, more productive interactions that are meaningful and impactful.

To wield the power of body language successfully, continuous observation and practice are essential. Mirror practice, role-playing, and feedback from peers can help refine your physical communication until it becomes an ally you employ with precision and confidence. Just as words are chosen carefully, so must your bodily expressions be curated to convey the intended meaning.

In mastering the influence of body language, you unlock the potential to engage, persuade, and connect with others on a deeply intrinsic level. This silent language speaks to the core of human interaction, enhancing your ability to communicate effectively across various fields and throughout different stages of life. Ultimately, understanding and harnessing body language bridges the gap between mere communication and true connection.

Reading Nonverbal Cues

In a world teeming with words, it's easy to overlook the symphony of signals we broadcast without uttering a single syllable. Yet, these nonverbal cues form a potent part of our daily communication, silently steering conversations and influencing impressions. Body language, facial expressions, and even the space between us and others play crucial roles in conveying messages that words alone can't capture. Recognizing and interpreting these nonverbal signs can significantly enhance our interactions, allowing us to connect with others at a deeper and more intuitive level.

Imagine two colleagues engaged in a discussion. One shares an innovative idea, punctuated by enthusiastic gestures and a warm smile. The other listens, arms crossed, lips pursed, eyes wandering. The words exchanged might sound amiable, but their body language tells a different story. The first is open and engaged; the latter is possibly skeptical or disinterested. By paying attention to these signals, we can adjust our approach, ask deeper questions, and ensure that genuine understanding takes place.

Nonverbal communication is universal, cutting across linguistic and cultural barriers. A nod of approval, a wave of dismissal, or a frown of discontent—these gestures are understood whether you're in Tokyo or Toronto. However, while certain expressions are globally recognized, many are nuanced or culturally specific. For instance, maintaining eye contact might denote confidence in some cultures, while in others, it could be seen as a challenge. Appreciating these subtleties helps us navigate interactions with more cultural sensitivity and awareness.

Facial expressions are perhaps the most overt of these cues, universally recognized and impactful. A genuine smile can light up a conversation, making the person feel at ease and understood. On the flip side, a furrowed brow or a tightened jaw can signal unease or disagreement. Researchers have identified a set of basic emotions—joy, anger, surprise, sadness, fear, and disgust—that are consistently expressed through similar facial cues across cultures. By observing these expressions, we can infer a person's emotional state, even if their words suggest otherwise.

But it's not just the face that's expressive. The position and movement of our bodies are also laden with meaning. Open postures, with arms uncrossed and legs placed firmly on the ground, often signal receptivity and engagement. In contrast, defensive or closed postures might indicate discomfort or resistance. Mirroring, where individuals subtly imitate each other's posture and movements, can also be a powerful indicator of rapport. This unconscious mimicry fosters trust and suggests a harmonious connection between the parties involved.

Proxemics, or the study of personal space, offers insight into our comfort levels and boundaries. Edward T. Hall, a pioneer in this field, categorized distances into four main zones: intimate, personal, social, and public. These zones vary from culture to culture. For example, someone from a densely populated city might feel comfortable standing closer in social settings than someone from a rural area. Being mindful of personal space can prevent unintentional invasion, which could make interactions awkward or strained. Respecting these boundaries is crucial for ensuring comfort and harmony.

Another valuable nonverbal cue is touch. A handshake, a pat on the back, or a gentle touch on the arm can communicate warmth, support, or encouragement. However, inappropriate or unexpected touch can lead to discomfort or misinterpretation. It's vital to be sensitive to the context and the other person's reaction to touch, especially in professional settings. Harnessing the power of appropriate touch can fortify bonds and enhance the sincerity of the message being conveyed.

The eyes, often described as the windows to the soul, offer another dimension of nonverbal communication. They can reveal enthusiasm, deception, or boredom. An engaged listener makes eye contact, glancing naturally at the speaker, while a person who's uninterested might frequently look away or check their watch or phone. Averting your gaze during a conversation might suggest nervousness or dishonesty. Mastering the art of appropriate eye contact—neither too intense nor too fleeting—ensures that the message you want to deliver is received with clarity and authenticity.

Voice modulation is an often-overlooked aspect of nonverbal communication, carrying with it the power to change the essence of any message. The tone, pitch, and speed of our speech can convey excitement, authority, or hesitation. A warm, steady voice builds confidence and invites engagement, while a monotone or rushed delivery might lead listeners to disengage or misinterpret the speaker's intent. By being mindful of vocal cues, we can enhance the impact of our spoken words and ensure they resonate more effectively with our audience.

To effectively read nonverbal cues, one must cultivate an acute sense of observation. This involves not only watching but truly seeing—understanding the unspoken messages others send and considering them alongside verbal communication. Paying attention to inconsistencies between words and body language can alert us to hidden feelings or intentions. For instance, someone may verbally agree while their body subtly indicates reluctance, giving us an opportunity to delve deeper and address underlying concerns.

Improving our sensitivity to these cues requires practice and a conscious effort to tune into others. Engaging in exercises like mirroring the body language of trusted friends during conversations or consciously observing facial expressions during casual interactions can enhance our ability to pick up on nonverbal signals. With time, we become attuned to these cues, allowing us to respond more intuitively in conversations, ultimately forging stronger and more meaningful connections.

Understanding and interpreting nonverbal communication isn't about becoming a mind reader; it's about being an attentive and empathetic communicator. The more we embrace these skills, the more adept we become at navigating the complexities of human interaction. This awareness doesn't just elevate our personal and professional relationships; it transforms the very fabric of how we communicate, turning dialogue into a more harmonious and holistic experience. By weaving together the threads of verbal and nonverbal communication, we form a tapestry that enriches every interaction, making us not only better communicators but better human beings.

Chapter 4: The Art of Active Listening

Active listening is more than just nodding along while someone speaks; it's about fully engaging with the speaker, understanding the message behind the words, and responding thoughtfully. By honing this skill, you open the door to more meaningful interactions and foster connections that go beyond surface-level exchanges. It's an art that requires patience, empathy, and self-awareness, every bit as important as the eloquence of your own speech. The techniques of active listening can help you break down barriers, turning potential misunderstandings into opportunities for deeper understanding. When you master the nuances of attentive listening, you'll not only become a better communicator but also a catalyst for collaboration and mutual respect in both personal and professional realms. This chapter invites you to explore how active listening can transform your communication style and, ultimately, your relationships.

Techniques for Better Listening

In the intricate dance of communication, listening often takes a backseat to speaking. Yet, to truly engage and connect with others, honing effective listening skills is paramount. Active listening isn't merely about passively receiving words; it's an art that requires attention, empathy, and a readiness to engage. Let's delve into some transformative techniques that can make the difference between a superficial exchange and a profound connection.

First and foremost, *presence* is key. Being present means dedicating your full attention to the speaker, both mentally and physically. This involves more than just hearing the words being spoken. When you're engaged, you're not formulating your next response or checking your phone. You're in tune with the conversation's ebb and flow, giving your conversation partner the gift of undivided attention.

Maintaining eye contact is a simple yet powerful tool to ensure presence. It shows that you're engaged and interested, helping to build trust and rapport. People naturally feel more valued and understood when they know they have your full attention. However, it's crucial to strike a balance. Too much eye contact can be overwhelming, while too little might make you seem disinterested. Finding that middle ground where you make others feel seen and heard is critical.

Another technique is **mirroring and paraphrasing**. By mirroring, you subtly imitate the speaker's expressions or words, which creates a subconscious bond. Paraphrasing involves rephrasing what the speaker has said in your own words. This not only shows that you're listening but also clarifies and confirms your understanding. It prevents miscommunications and ensures that you're both on the same page.

Asking open-ended questions is another effective listening strategy. They encourage expansive dialogue rather than just yes or no answers. When you ask questions that require reflection and elaboration, you create space for the speaker to express deeper thoughts and feelings. This not only enriches the conversation but fosters a deeper connection between you and the speaker.

Practicing empathy, or trying to understand the speaker's perspective and emotional state, is at the heart of active listening. This requires patience and an open mind. Empathy allows you to connect with the speaker on a deeper level, recognizing their emotions and validating their experiences. You don't have to agree, but showing that you understand can be incredibly powerful.

Nonverbal cues play an essential role in effective listening. Nodding occasionally, maintaining a relaxed posture, and offering appropriate gestures demonstrate your attentiveness and understanding. These small, often unconscious signs communicate interest and receptivity, reinforcing the words and emotions being exchanged.

It's also important to manage **internal distractions**. Our minds are often racing with thoughts, but recognizing when this happens and gently bringing your focus back to the present is crucial in active listening. One technique is to silently repeat the speaker's key points in your mind, which helps anchor your attention and keeps distractions at bay.

Sometimes, silence is golden. Allowing pauses in a conversation can provide the speaker room to think and expand on their thoughts. It indicates that you're comfortable with reflection and allows you both to contemplate what's being said. Silence can often encourage more profound insights by offering the speaker a moment to gather their thoughts.

Feedback is an aspect of listening that shouldn't be overlooked. Responding with thoughtful comments that build on the speaker's points shows active engagement. This doesn't mean interrupting, but rather waiting for natural pauses to offer your reflections or questions. It highlights your involvement in the conversation and demonstrates that you value their input.

Taking care of your own emotional state is vital when listening. Being aware of your biases and preconceptions can prevent them from interfering with the communication process. By monitoring your reactions and managing emotional triggers, you maintain a more open and receptive mindset.

Finally, embracing the concept of **nonjudgmental listening** helps keep conversations open and constructive. When you let go of judgments or preconceived ideas about the speaker or their message, you allow the conversation to flow freely and authentically. This openness can lead to discovering insights and perspectives that might otherwise be missed.

In the journey to become a better listener, these techniques offer a guiding framework to strengthen our communication skills. Active listening fosters a deeper understanding and connection with others, paving the way for meaningful and impactful interactions. Embrace these techniques in your daily conversations, and witness the transformative power of genuine, attentive listening.

Overcoming Listening Barriers

In the intricate dance of communication, listening is an essential partner often overshadowed by the more glamorous counterpart—speaking. Yet, the art of active listening is not simply about remaining silent while the other person talks; it's about overcoming the myriad barriers that impede our ability to truly understand and connect with others. These barriers are as varied as they are pervasive, ranging from the physical to the psychological, and they challenge our capacity to listen effectively.

One of the most common listening barriers we encounter is the pervasive presence of distractions. In our modern world, full of buzzing smartphones, incoming emails, and the cacophony of everyday life, it can be a struggle to focus our minds entirely on the person speaking. The first step in overcoming this barrier is cultivating an awareness of the distractions around us and making a conscious effort to minimize them. This may mean setting aside our devices during conversations and turning off notifications to prioritize the human interaction happening in front of us.

Another significant barrier is preconceived notions and personal biases. Our own beliefs, experiences, and judgments can cloud our listening, creating a filter through which the speaker's message is distorted or selectively heard. To overcome this, it's crucial to approach each conversation with an open mind, recognizing that our initial assumptions might be flawed. Doing so requires humility and a genuine curiosity to learn from others, rather than merely confirming what we think we already know.

Emotional triggers can also obstruct our ability to listen effectively. Certain topics or phrases can evoke strong emotional responses, which may prevent us from fully processing what is being said. In these moments, practicing emotional regulation is key. It's important to pause, take a breath, and refocus on the speaker's words, reminding ourselves of the larger goal of understanding their perspective. It can be helpful to ask for clarification, which not only aids our comprehension but also signals to the speaker our commitment to engaging with their message.

The barrier of superficial listening is often a result of our natural inclination to focus on what we're going to say next, rather than on the content being delivered to us. This tendency to prepare our response before the other person has finished speaking hinders true understanding. To counteract this habit, it can be beneficial to practice active listening techniques such as paraphrasing what the speaker has said and asking pertinent questions. These strategies not only demonstrate engagement but reinforce our memory and understanding of the conversation's key points.

One can't overlook the impact of physiological barriers, such as hearing impairments or fatigue, which can interfere with effective listening. Overcoming these requires both self-awareness and proactive measures. If one is tired or unwell, acknowledging this state and, if possible, rescheduling important conversations can lead to better outcomes. For hearing difficulties, using assistive devices or optimizing the environment for better acoustics can greatly improve the listening experience.

Listeners also face the challenge of information overload in a world where we are bombarded with data at every turn. This excess can numb our ability to absorb and process information, leading to reduced retention and comprehension during discussions. To manage this, it may be necessary to filter out unnecessary information and focus on the most critical aspects of the conversation. Taking notes can also be a practical way to manage complex information and ensure that we remain engaged.

Overcoming listening barriers is not simply a matter of addressing external causes; it also involves a certain degree of introspection. Reflecting on our own listening habits and recognizing patterns that hinder our ability to connect with others is essential for personal growth. By acknowledging our strengths and areas for improvement, we empower ourselves to make conscious changes that enhance our overall effectiveness as communicators.

But perhaps the most profound barrier to listening is the absence of genuine empathy. Without empathy, listening becomes a transactional process devoid of real connection. To truly overcome listening barriers, we must cultivate the ability to put ourselves in others' shoes and understand not just their words, but the emotions and intentions behind them. This requires patience, compassion, and the willingness to embrace the vulnerability that comes with deep listening.

In conclusion, overcoming listening barriers is a multifaceted endeavor that demands intentionality and practice. By recognizing and addressing the distractions, biases, emotional triggers, and physiological limitations we face, we pave the way for clearer, more meaningful communication. The journey to becoming a more effective listener is ongoing, but with perseverance, we can transform our interactions and forge deeper connections with those around us.

Chapter 5: Crafting Your Message

In the delicate art of communication, the words we choose aren't just carriers of information; they're bridges to understanding and tools of influence. Crafting your message with precision and clarity is a strategic endeavor that requires awareness of both the audience and the context. It involves selecting words that resonate, structuring sentences for maximum impact, and ensuring that every phrase aligns with the intended emotional tone. This process taps into the psychology of how people perceive and are persuaded, emphasizing the power of nuanced language tailored to connect on deeper levels. Balancing simplicity with sophistication, the art of message crafting is as much about what you say as how you say it, creating a tapestry of understanding that encourages connection, prompts action, and leaves a lasting impression. As you refine your ability to craft compelling messages, you don't just communicate—you captivate and inspire transformation.

The Importance of Word Choice

In the realm of communication, the words we choose carry tremendous power. Whether you're crafting a persuasive speech, sending an email, or having a casual conversation, the language you use can significantly influence how your message is perceived and whether it achieves its intended purpose. Words are not just tools; they are the bridge between your thoughts and the external world. They have the ability to inspire action, evoke emotion, and build understanding.

A well-thought-out word choice can transform a simple statement into a compelling narrative. Consider how marketers use language to evoke emotions in potential customers. They don't just describe a product's features; they use words that conjure images of improved lifestyles and fulfilled dreams. This is why brands spend millions on crafting the perfect tagline—it encapsulates their message and appeals to the audience's emotions, driving engagement and, ultimately, action.

But it isn't just in advertising where word choice matters. Take diplomacy, for example. Diplomats spend hours crafting statements with precise wording, because a single phrase can be the difference between peace and tension. Similarly, in everyday personal interactions, the words we select can prevent misunderstandings and foster stronger relations.

Choosing the right words requires a deep understanding of both your message and your audience. It's about asking yourself: "What am I really trying to say?", "What reaction do I want to evoke?", and "How can my word choice reflect empathy and respect for my audience?" This reflection is integral to effective communication, whether you're writing, speaking, or even texting.

Moreover, the connotations that particular words carry can greatly impact how a sentence is understood. Words with positive connotations can elevate a message, while those with negative undertones might dilute or distort it. Think about words like "challenge" versus "problem"; the former suggests an opportunity for growth, while the latter might imply a hindrance. This is a subtle yet powerful distinction that can define the tone of your communication.

Language isn't static. It evolves with cultural shifts, new trends, and technological advances. English today bears little resemblance to that of a century ago, not just in vocabulary but also in usage and style. Keeping up with this evolution allows communicators to remain relevant and relatable. It's crucial to adapt and embrace new expressions while remaining mindful of traditional nuances that shape discourse.

An essential aspect of word choice is brevity. In a world inundated with information, being concise can be a distinguishing factor. Aim to express your thoughts as clearly and economically as possible. Trim the excess without compromising the core message. However, this doesn't mean stripping away complexity where needed. Complex ideas often demand richer language. The key is balance.

Precision in language also counters ambiguity. Ambiguity can be the nemesis of effective communication. It muddles the message and leaves room for misinterpretation. For instance, when giving feedback, vague comments are less helpful than specific ones. Instead of saying "You need to improve your performance," consider "Your project management skills could benefit from more detailed planning." Specificity not only clarifies the message but also guides actionable improvements.

Furthermore, inclusive language is vital in our diverse world. Word choice can either recognize diverse identities and experiences or unintentionally alienate. Strive for language that acknowledges and respects differences, fostering an environment conducive to connection and understanding. Terms matter, and so does the graceful navigation of pronouns and descriptors.

It's also important to tailor your word choice to match the context and medium. What works in a face-to-face conversation might not be suitable for an email. In written communication, where tone and body language are absent, words bear the brunt of the message. They need to compensate for this lack of nonverbal cues, ensuring clarity and understanding.

In practice, refining your word choice takes time and conscious effort. It involves not just expanding your vocabulary but also honing your instinct for speech and writing. The journey to mastering language is ongoing, marked by both successes and lessons learned from missteps. Reading widely, listening actively, and reflecting on feedback all sharpen linguistic skills, enhancing your ability to choose words wisely.

Ultimately, effective word choice is one pillar of successful communication. While the choice of words is crucial, it works in concert with tone, cadence, and context to shape the clarity and impact of your message. By paying attention to the power of your words, you can improve not just what you say but also how it's received, leading to more profound and lasting connections.

Remember, every word counts. So, wield them carefully, with intention and precision. Whether your goal is to persuade, inform, or entertain, the words you choose will always be your most influential ally.

Structuring Your Message

When it comes to effective communication, the structure of your message is just as important as its content. Imagine trying to build a house without a blueprint. The materials might be high-quality, but without a proper structure, they won't come together to create a cohesive whole. The same goes for communication; it's not just about what you say but how you say it. Structuring your message gives clarity and impact, ensuring your audience not only understands but also engages with your ideas.

Every well-structured message starts with a clear purpose. Before you even begin crafting your message, ask yourself: What is the desired outcome? Are you trying to inform, persuade, entertain, or instruct? Having a precise goal in mind guides the organization of your thoughts and provides a north star for your communication journey. A clear purpose keeps your message on track, preventing it from meandering and losing its effectiveness.

Once you've nailed down the purpose, it's time to consider the audience. Different audiences require different approaches. For instance, communicating a complex idea to experts in a field may require a different structure than explaining the same idea to novices. Tailoring your message's structure to your audience's needs and expectations makes it more relatable and digestible. Understanding who you're speaking to is crucial—it's like knowing the language of your listener, ensuring your message hits home.

One of the most crucial elements of structuring your message is the beginning. The opening sets the tone and hooks your audience's attention. Whether it's a startling statistic, a compelling question, or a brief story, the introduction should engage your audience's curiosity and encourage them to stay with you until the end. A strong opening acts like a magnet, drawing your listeners or readers into the heart of what you want to convey.

After grabbing attention with your opening, it's vital to transition smoothly into the core of your message. Here, coherence is key. Logical organization aids comprehension. Consider the story arc: a beginning, middle, and end. Just as a story unfolds in a sequence, your message should follow a similar path. Each part of your message should build upon the last, seamlessly guiding your audience through your points.

Breaking down your message into smaller, manageable sections can significantly enhance its clarity. Think of these sections as building blocks, each representing a point you wish to make. These blocks should be logically connected, supporting the overall purpose of your message. For instance, when making a persuasive argument, you might present a problem, explore its implications, and then offer a solution. This logical progression helps your audience not only follow your train of thought but also arrive at the conclusion you've drawn.

Within these sections, the choice of words plays a pivotal role. Use language that's appropriate for your audience but also rich in imagery and emotion to paint a picture of your ideas. Your word choice can elevate the message, transforming abstract concepts into tangible images that resonate with your listeners or readers. Descriptive language adds color and depth, helping your audience visualize and feel what you're communicating.

Transitions between sections are the unsung heroes of message structure. They serve as bridges, ensuring that the flow of ideas is seamless and natural. Without them, even well-thought-out points can feel disjointed. A well-placed transition keeps your audience oriented, guiding them smoothly from one idea to the next. It's the difference between a harmonious melody and a jarring sequence of notes.

Equally important in structuring your message is the end—it should be resolute and memorable. Whether the aim is to inform, persuade, or entertain, leave your audience with a takeaway that lingers long after the conversation has ended. A strong conclusion reinforces your main points and invites reflection or action. Consider using a call to action, a rhetorical question, or a poignant statement that echoes your initial purpose.

Feedback loops are an essential component of adjusting and enhancing your message structure. Once you've crafted your message, seek feedback to gain insights into how it is received. Does the audience grasp the main points? Are they left with questions? Use this information to fine-tune your structure for clarity and impact. The process of crafting your message is iterative, allowing continuous improvements towards perfection.

While strong emotional appeal can significantly enhance your message, balance is key. Emotional elements should complement the logical structure, not overshadow it. This harmony ensures that while your audience is emotionally engaged, they also understand and remember the core ideas you wish to communicate. Emotional engagement coupled with solid structure creates a holistic message that resonates deeply.

In summary, structuring your message is an art that combines purpose, audience awareness, logical progression, and emotional resonance. By focusing on these elements, you can craft communication that's not just heard, but truly understood and remembered. As you hone these skills, you'll find that your ability to connect, persuade, and impact others grows exponentially. The craft of communication is ever-evolving, and with every message you structure, you enhance your capacity to influence and inspire the world around you.

Chapter 6: Building Rapport

Creating genuine connections with others often hinges on our ability to build rapport, a critical skill that transcends simple conversation. At its core, building rapport is about establishing a harmonious relationship characterized by trust and understanding, which enables one to communicate more effectively and persuasively. To initiate this, it's essential to engage in active listening, showing genuine interest in the other person's perspective and emotions, which fosters a sense of validation and respect. By mirroring body language naturally and using empathetic language, you can subtly signal alignment with the other person's values and feelings. This, in turn, cultivates an environment where trust can flourish and dialogues become more open and sincere. While it may seem intangible, rapport isn't a mysterious art but a skill that can be nurtured through consistent practice and awareness. By harnessing these techniques, you not only pave the way for more successful interactions but also enrich your personal and professional relationships, making them more resilient and fulfilling.

Psychological Strategies for Connection

At the heart of building rapport lies a suite of psychological strategies that can transform interactions from mundane exchanges to rich connections. Humans are inherently social beings, and the quality of our interactions often determines our personal and professional success. It's more than just talking; it's about understanding the unspoken dance of psychology that happens within every conversation. Establishing a genuine connection requires an insightful blend of empathy, authenticity, and psychological awareness. The trick is to connect without coming across as overbearing or disingenuous.

One of the first strategies is recognizing and leveraging the power of mirroring. This involves subtly copying the behavior of the person you're engaging with, such as matching their body language, tone of voice, or even breathing patterns. This unconscious mimicry can foster a sense of familiarity and comfort, many times leading to stronger rapport. It's an art form rather than a science, requiring sensitivity to the other person's cues. You don't want it to be obvious; rather, it's about naturally syncing up your behavior to create an invisible bond.

Empathy acts as a cornerstone for many successful connections. It's the ability to genuinely understand and feel another person's emotions. Yet, empathy is not merely about nodding along; it requires active engagement. An empathetic listener doesn't just listen to what's being said but also seeks to understand what isn't. By tuning into emotional cues, you become attuned to another's emotional state, offering responses that are both supportive and validating. This doesn't mean you have to agree with everything the other person says, but understanding their perspective is crucial.

Another critical psychological strategy is the effective use of questions. Asking open-ended, thoughtful questions invites deeper dialogue and shows the other person that you truly care about their thoughts and experiences. This technique naturally draws people out, making them more receptive to communication and more inclined to trust. Questions that explore feelings, motivations, and aspirations can shift the focus away from surface-level topics, giving way to more meaningful conversations. But remember, the key is active listening. Asking questions without genuinely listening defeats the purpose.

Authenticity is a vital component in establishing rapport. People are perceptive to disingenuity. Genuine interactions are built on honesty and sincerity. When you express yourself truthfully, it encourages others to open up with equal candor. Authenticity often breaks down defensive barriers, allowing for a more genuine connection. Yet, being genuine doesn't mean oversharing or being bluntly honest inappropriately; it's about aligning your words and actions consistently with who you are.

Moreover, the psychological principle of reciprocity can be pivotal. This principle refers to the social norm of responding to a positive action with another positive action. Offering small gestures of goodwill or kindness, whether through compliments or acts of service, can encourage a sense of obligation or appreciation in return. This isn't about manipulation; it's about fostering a mutual sense of giving and receiving, which can powerfully strengthen ties between individuals.

Personal anecdotes and storytelling are also strategic devices for creating connections. Sharing personal stories not only makes you more relatable but also humanizes interactions. Stories have the power to elicit emotional responses, bridging gaps between different perspectives and experiences. Storytelling encourages vulnerability and intimacy, which are essential elements of strong rapport. Balance is key here; while sharing can build connection, dominating the conversation with personal tales might alienate others. The art lies in knowing what to share and when to share it.

Lastly, fostering trust through consistency and reliability cannot be overstated. Trust is the cornerstone of any meaningful relationship, built through consistent actions over time. This means following through on promises, being punctual, and demonstrating reliability in small ways. Trust grows from predictability in behavior, offering a stable ground upon which deeper connections can be forged.

In the pursuit of connection, it's important to remember that building rapport is a dynamic and ongoing process. Each interaction is a unique tapestry of psychological undercurrents, emotions, and social dynamics. The more you practice these strategies, the more innate they become, allowing you to connect on a deeper level with those around you. Successful communication hinges upon the ability to understand and apply these psychological strategies thoughtfully, truly paving the way for meaningful and enriching human connections.

Maintaining Trust and Credibility

In any interaction, trust is the bridge that connects individuals and fosters real rapport. It is a cornerstone of meaningful relationships, whether in personal life or the professional realm. Trust is not built overnight; it's cultivated with intention and care. Credibility, closely linked, is about how others perceive our reliability and integrity. Together, they create a foundation for successful communication.

Maintaining trust requires consistency. A person who shows up, as promised, is someone others will rely upon. When our actions align with our words, we project authenticity. It's the small, everyday acts that build this sense of consistency. From returning phone calls to following through on promises, these actions strengthen the perception of reliability. Over time, these behaviors contribute to a solid reputation.

However, we all face moments that test our ability to maintain credibility. Mistakes can happen. When they do, how we handle them is crucial. Owning up to errors, apologizing sincerely, and correcting course whenever necessary showcases maturity. Authenticity in these moments, admitting when you don't know an answer and showing a willingness to learn, adds layers to your credibility.

Building credibility also involves displaying competence. Competence isn't just about having the right knowledge or skills. It's about demonstrating them effectively in situations that matter. When you're able to articulate ideas clearly and understand different perspectives, it becomes easier for others to see you as a competent communicator. This perception fosters confidence in your ability to engage effectively.

Trust is further affirmed through transparency. Transparency in communication dispels potential for misunderstanding and fosters a sense of security. When we're open about goals, challenges, and intentions, we invite others into our world. This openness encourages reciprocal behavior, leading to more profound, more trusting exchanges. Moreover, transparency can build a safer environment where authentic dialogue thrives.

Yet, transparency doesn't equate to oversharing. There's an art to balancing vulnerability with discretion. It's about knowing when transparency aids understanding and when it risks compromising personal boundaries or confidentiality. This balance is where we exhibit judgment and sensitivity, valuable traits when fostering rapport and trust.

Another crucial facet of maintaining trust and credibility is empathy. When we listen with genuine interest and respond with understanding, we validate others' emotions and perspectives. This validation is a powerful tool in acknowledging the humanity in our interactions. When people feel understood, they're more likely to trust and open up, further facilitating genuine connection.

While empathy builds an emotional bond, consistency in behavior sustains it. The most impactful communicators consistently exhibit respect, honesty, and integrity. By nurturing these qualities, we create a workplace or a personal environment characterized by openness and mutual respect. It's this consistency that makes others feel secure in our interactions, knowing they can depend on our words and actions.

Furthermore, understanding the dynamic nature of trust is key. Trust isn't a static concept; it evolves. Situations change, and relationships mature. As they do, maintaining trust means adapting and showing flexibility when needed. Being attuned to these shifts helps in managing expectations and staying aligned with those we engage with.

Additionally, maintaining credibility necessitates mindful communication. The words we choose carry weight. Language, tone, and delivery shape how messages are received and interpreted. Being conscious of these elements ensures our communication is as effective and impactful as possible, enhancing our reliability in others' eyes.

In the digital age, upholding trust and credibility presents new challenges. Online interactions lack the visual and vocal nuances of face-to-face conversation, making consistent behavior and tone even more critical. Ensuring clarity and appropriateness in our digital communication reinforces our reliability and trustworthiness.

Finally, seek feedback as a tool for maintaining trust and building credibility. Regularly asking for input helps you understand how others perceive your actions and words. This feedback loop supports personal growth and refinement in how you communicate and interact, allowing you to stay aligned with those you wish to build trustworthy relationships with.

In summary, trust and credibility are vital to sustaining rapport in our interactions. They're nurtured through consistent actions, humility in facing mistakes, effective demonstration of skills, transparency balanced with discretion, empathetic engagement, and mindful communication. While technology transforms the landscape of communication, these timeless principles remain, guiding us to create genuine and lasting connections with others.

Chapter 7: Communicating with Influence

In the dynamic world of human interaction, the ability to communicate with influence is a transformative skill that bridges intention and impact. At its core, influential communication requires a deep understanding of not just what to say, but how to say it to resonate on an emotional and psychological level. It marries the logic of structured messaging with the art of empathy and connection, creating a platform where ideas don't just reach ears—they penetrate hearts. Employing persuasion techniques becomes vital, as does the capacity to weave narratives that inspire and drive action while navigating through resistance with grace and confidence. When you master this balance, you become a catalyst for change, capable of motivating others and cultivating relationships rooted in trust and authenticity. Bustling beneath the surface of effective influence is a strategic coordination of words, tone, and presence, crafted meticulously to not just convey a message but to transform perspectives. With these tools, one can harness the profound ability to leave a lasting impression, guiding conversations toward meaningful and mutually beneficial outcomes.

Persuasion Techniques

When we dive into the realm of persuasion, we navigate the crossroads where communication and influence meet. Persuasive communication isn't just about getting others to adopt your ideas; it's about creating a connection so genuine and transparent that the listener feels not only engaged but motivated to respond. At its core, persuasion is a cultivated skill—one that hinges on understanding the psychological undercurrents of human interaction.

To truly persuade, the key lies in tapping into intrinsic motivations. We're driven by desires, fears, and aspirations. Good persuaders understand this well, crafting their message in a way that resonates on a deeper level. Whether in professional settings or personal relationships, the art lies in aligning what you propose with the desires or solves the concerns of your audience. It's about painting a picture of a future state that's too compelling to ignore.

But why does persuasion work with some and not others? A huge factor is credibility. Are you believed? Do your listeners trust your intentions? Establishing credibility right from the start is essential. This can be achieved through demonstrating expertise, showcasing genuine empathy, or even sharing personal stories that resonate with the audience's experiences. The key is to be authentic. The moment authenticity is compromised, persuasion falls apart.

Aside from credibility, reciprocation plays a significant role. This operates on the principle that people feel obliged to return favors. Offering something of value—perhaps a piece of advice, a compliment, or a small favor—creates a subtle psychological debt. This doesn't imply manipulation; rather, it's the human tendency to match generosity with generosity. The more authentic and generous the gesture, the more likely it is to elicit a positive response.

Another powerful tool lies in social proof. Gamely said, we are social creatures, often looking to others to guide our actions. This means showcasing endorsements, testimonials, or simply sharing anecdotes of others who've benefited from your perspective. It provides assurance that others have tread that path and found it rewarding. Humans find comfort in numbers, and seeing others validate a message makes it that much more persuasive.

Commitment and consistency principles also drive persuasion. Once someone has committed—verbally or nonverbally—they are more likely to stick to it. This stems from a psychological desire to be consistent in our words and actions. Therefore, gently encouraging initial small agreements can lead to bigger commitments, as people naturally avoid cognitive dissonance by aligning subsequent actions with their previous commitments.

Let's not overlook the power of scarcity. Constructing an environment where opportunities are seen as limited or exclusive can enhance perceived value. People tend to place higher value on things that appear hard to attain. It taps into the fear of missing out, sparking a sense of urgency. However, ethical considerations should guide the use of scarcity to prevent exploitative practices.

Contrary to what some may believe, emotion often outweighs logic in the persuasion game. While rational arguments are important, it's the emotional connection that truly sways decisions. Storytelling emerges as an invaluable tool here. Through stories, persuaders can evoke emotions, transport audiences and create empathy. This emotional resonance often leads to a stronger persuasive impact than sheer data ever could.

Now, consider timing. The when of persuasion can be just as crucial as the what. Attentiveness to the right moment can make or break the persuasive effort. Engaging someone when they're open-minded and receptive can dramatically increase success rates. This often means understanding your audience's mood, context, and current challenges, then tailoring your approach to fit their present state.

Language also plays its role. Word choice can amplify or dampen the persuasive power of a message. Words brim with connotations, and tapping into those that carry positive, action-oriented, or vivid imagery will often yield better results. The way words are structured, their rhythm, and even their tone contribute to the persuasive effectiveness. The art lies in weaving words into a coherent, impactful narrative that speaks directly to the heart of your audience.

It's crucial to address potential objections upfront. Anticipating areas of resistance allows you to pre-emptively counteract them, thus maintaining the flow of persuasion. Addressing doubts openly demonstrates not only foresight but also respect for the audience's intelligence. It signals that the communicator has done their homework, is transparent, and genuinely seeks a mutual understanding.

Finally, never underestimate the importance of listening as part of persuasion. Real persuasion isn't a monologue; it's a dance that involves active, respectful engagement. By listening intently to the concerns and aspirations of others, you glean insights that inform your approach. It ensures that the conversation feels more collaborative than coercive, creating a space where ideas can flourish and persuasion is a natural evolution of the dialogue.

Mastering persuasion involves a manifold appreciation of human nature, communication dynamics, and ethical grounding. It's about nurturing relationships, building connections, and, ultimately, inspiring change. It's the art of influencing not just through words, but through presence, empathy, and authenticity. Remember, the ultimate goal is to create a shared vision that benefits all involved, fostered through respect, understanding, and genuine enthusiasm.

Overcoming Resistance

One of the central challenges in communicating with influence is overcoming resistance. Resistance can manifest in many ways—skepticism, denial, outright opposition—and it can derail even the most thoughtfully crafted messages. To communicate effectively and yield the desired impact, it's essential to understand what fuels resistance and develop strategies to counteract it.

Resistance often stems from deeply ingrained beliefs and values that do not align with the communicator's message. These beliefs act as mental filters, through which the recipient processes information. If the message does not fit the established narrative within those filters, it may be dismissed. To overcome this, one must first understand the audience's perspective and the values they hold dear. This understanding enables the communicator to frame the message in a way that resonates with the audience's belief system, rather than clashing with it.

The initial step in this process is active listening. By truly listening, one can uncover the core reasons behind resistance. It may be fear of change, lack of trust, or past experiences that influence current perceptions. Addressing these underlying factors requires empathy and genuine engagement. Imagine an open dialogue where the goal is not to impose but to align interests.

Timing plays a crucial role in overcoming resistance. Introducing an idea when the audience is not ready can result in immediate rejection. The key is to look for opportune moments when the audience is more open to new ideas—perhaps when they are seeking solutions to a problem or when external circumstances have led to a shift in perspective. This is why flexibility in communication strategy is vital. Being attuned to the right moment can enhance receptivity.

Creating small wins can also pave the way in reducing resistance to larger ideas. When individuals see tangible benefits from gradual changes, they become more amenable to embracing bigger concepts. An effective communicator identifies these opportunities to build momentum and guide the audience through incremental acceptance. It's about fostering an environment where openness and curiosity toward new ideas are encouraged.

Credibility significantly influences how messages are received. If the audience perceives the communicator as trustworthy and knowledgeable, they are more likely to engage with the message, regardless of initial reservations. Establishing trust involves consistent actions that demonstrate integrity and reliability. Credibility is not built overnight but is the result of sustained, transparent communication.

Another technique is to harness the power of storytelling. Compelling narratives have the unique ability to bypass logical resistance, appealing directly to emotions. Stories create a connection that facts and data alone often cannot. They allow the audience to visualize themselves within the scenario, experiencing the potential outcomes of resisting or embracing the communicated concept. Carefully chosen stories can shift perceptions and dismantle barriers.

On another note, resistance is sometimes fueled by a lack of perceived benefit or relevance. This is where clarity in communication becomes indispensable. The message must clearly articulate what is at stake and highlight the benefits in a manner that directly relates to the audience's goals and aspirations. Emphasizing relevance ensures that the audience understands why the message matters to them personally or professionally.

In any encounter with resistance, it is crucial to maintain patience and persistence. Resistance is not always a sign of rejection—it can indicate that the audience needs more information, time, or a different perspective before they are ready to accept new ideas. Through perseverance and consistent engagement, resistance can gradually be transformed into understanding and ultimately, support.

For this transformation to occur, feedback mechanisms are invaluable. Encouraging open dialogue where feedback is not only welcomed but sought after allows the communicator to adjust their approach and steer the conversation in a more productive direction. Feedback, when leveraged effectively, can illuminate blind spots and provide insights into what may need to change in the message or delivery to reduce resistance.

Moreover, aligning the message with the audience's identity can diminish resistance. When individuals feel that an idea reinforces their self-concept or personal narrative, they are more likely to embrace it. This requires a nuanced approach, identifying aspects of the message that resonate with the audience's sense of self and emphasizing these connections throughout the communication process.

Lastly, embracing a spirit of collaboration rather than confrontation can significantly mitigate resistance. When individuals feel they are part of a collective effort, as opposed to mere recipients of information, they are more inclined to engage in meaningful dialogue and consider the merits of the message. Collaboration fosters mutual respect and opens the door to compromise and joint problem solving.

To conclude, overcoming resistance in communication is a multifaceted endeavor that requires a deep understanding of human psychology and an adaptable approach. By listening actively, understanding the audience's values, timing interventions wisely, and crafting messages that connect emotionally, it is possible to transform resistance into acceptance and cooperation. The journey isn't without its challenges, but the reward is a higher level of influence and more fruitful connections.

Chapter 8: Emotional Intelligence in Communication

In the intricate dance of human interaction, emotional intelligence serves as the rhythm that syncs thoughts and feelings, guiding our communication to resonate deeper with others. By honing the ability to recognize and understand emotions—not only our own but also those of the people we engage with—we unlock pathways to more meaningful and persuasive exchanges. This awareness allows us to manage our emotional responses, crafting our messages in ways that transcend words and touch on relational cores. Emotional intelligence doesn't merely enhance conversations; it transforms them. As we internalize these skills, we forge connections that can sway opinions, soothe conflicts, and inspire change, underpinning every successful communication endeavor with empathy and insight.

Understanding Emotions

Emotions are the rich, vibrant threads woven into the fabric of human communication. They fuel our interactions, influencing every word we choose and how we interpret the messages we receive. To truly understand emotions is to unlock a deeper, more genuine form of communication that can transform our relationships and interactions.

At its core, emotional intelligence begins with the ability to recognize, understand, and manage our own emotions and the emotions of others. This ability not only enhances personal growth but also boosts our capacity to engage effectively with others. When we grasp the dynamics of our emotions, we pave the way for clearer, more intentional dialogue. Instead of allowing emotions to unconsciously steer our interactions, we learn to channel them to enhance our communication.

Consider a moment when you've felt overwhelmed by emotion—perhaps anger during a heated debate or frustration in a misunderstanding. Such feelings can cloud judgment, making communication muddled or even aggressive. But by recognizing these emotions early, we gain the power to pause, reflect, and respond rather than react. This pause is not merely a hesitation but a purposeful choice to steer the conversation in a constructive direction.

Moreover, understanding emotions fosters empathy—a vital component in effective communication. Empathy allows us to step into another person's shoes, to feel their joys and struggles as our own. This emotional connection breaks down barriers, creating a space where open and honest dialogue can flourish.

In contrast, ignoring or suppressing emotions can be detrimental. It can lead to miscommunications and misunderstandings, as the authentic emotional context of a message is lost. People sense when something is off, when the emotional undertones don't match the spoken words. Thus, acknowledging emotions is not just a personal necessity but also a social skill that enhances our interactions.

Understanding emotions also holds the key to persuasion and influence. When we tune into the emotions of those we interact with, we can tailor our messages to more effectively resonate with them. We become adept at not just speaking but engaging—crafting conversations that appeal to the listener's emotional frameworks.

Further, our ability to navigate the complex terrain of emotions can greatly impact professional settings. In leadership, for instance, emotional intelligence is a cornerstone for inspiring and motivating teams. Leaders who understand and harness emotions can cultivate a supportive environment where team dynamics thrive, and collaboration becomes seamless.

Developing this skill calls for introspection and practice. One practical approach is the habit of reflecting on emotional responses to various situations—both personal and professional. By asking, "Why do I feel this way?" or "How might this person be feeling?" we begin to unravel emotional patterns and learn how to manage them productively.

Importantly, understanding emotions isn't about becoming someone else or suppressing natural feelings. It's about gaining control over how those emotions influence your actions and reactions. It teaches you to distinguish between emotions that serve a purpose and those that, if left unchecked, could mislead or harm relationships.

Additionally, this understanding builds resilience. By being emotionally aware, we can cope better with criticism or setbacks. Rather than spiraling into anxiety or anger, we can approach challenges with calmness and clarity. This resilience not only strengthens our personal resolve but also builds stronger, more flexible relationships with others.

In essence, genuine understanding of emotions prepares us for the myriad forms of communication we encounter daily—be it in family conversations, friendships, or professional dialogues. It's about creating harmony between what we feel and how we express these feelings effectively.

As we continue to explore emotional intelligence, it becomes clear that emotions, understood and harnessed correctly, become our greatest allies in the quest for meaningful communication. Through this lens, we view every interaction as an opportunity not only to convey thoughts but also to connect on a deeper emotional level. Such connections, made with intention and care, possess the power to enrich our lives and the lives of those we engage with.

Managing Emotional Responses

In the realms of effective communication, understanding and managing emotional responses isn't just a desirable asset; it's a necessity. Communication is not solely an exchange of words—it is an interchange of feelings, intentions, and perceptions. Mastering how we handle our emotions and deciphering those of others can dramatically improve the quality of our interactions and relationships.

The first step in managing emotional responses is self-awareness. This involves recognizing and understanding our own emotions—what they are, why they arise, and how they affect our communication patterns. By taking a moment to pause and reflect on your emotional state, you afford yourself the chance to respond rather than react. Successful communicators acknowledge this dynamic; they use it to craft responses that facilitate understanding rather than conflict.

While it's important to be prepared emotionally, it's equally necessary to remain flexible. Emotions have an unpredictable nature—they can escalate quickly, take unexpected turns, or reappear. Being emotionally flexible involves cultivating a mindset that is open to adapting your emotional responses to the nuances of each situation. Flexibility allows you to handle both adversities and opportunities with poise, promoting a stable foundation for dialog.

Active listening plays a pivotal role when engaging with someone who is emotional. Listening with empathy and without judgment not only provides support to others but also aids in defusing heightened emotions. Using appropriate body language, maintaining eye contact, and nodding are part of this approach, showing genuine interest and understanding. These nonverbal signals reinforce the belief that their feelings are both heard and valued.

Consider, for example, using specific language that names the emotions you're navigating. Phrases like "I sense that you're feeling upset" or "It seems like there's some frustration here" can validate the other person's experience, helping to defuse mounting tensions and demonstrating empathy. The ability to articulate emotions can transform an emotional dialogue into a constructive one, fostering a climate of mutual respect and understanding.

In managing emotions during communication, another key element to consider is the practice of mindfulness. Mindfulness involves being fully present in the moment, aware of but not overwhelmed by what's happening inside and around us. This presence not only helps in recognizing when emotions start to shift but also enables you to anchor your reactions in authentic engagement rather than knee-jerk responses.

When it comes to diffusing your own heightened emotions, remember that breathing exercises serve as a powerful tool. Taking slow, deliberate breaths can lower heart rates and provide much-needed patience. Such physiological cues can remind you that managing emotions is about embracing the moment rather than letting it dictate your behavior.

Moreover, reframing negative emotions creatively can act as an antidote to emotional challenges. It's about shifting your perception from seeing emotions as hurdles into opportunities for learning and growth. If a conversation evokes frustration, try viewing it as a signal of deeper engagement with the subject. This change in perspective can open up new avenues for problem-solving and collaboration.

Suppose an emotionally charged interaction spirals out of control. In that case, taking a break from the conversation can be incredibly beneficial. Stepping back from a situation allows you and the other party to cool down, reflect, and prepare to re-enter the discussion with more clarity and resolve. This doesn't mean running away from communications but taking a strategic pause to replenish emotional clarity.

Finally, embracing a positive outlook significantly impacts how emotions are managed in communication. By focusing on what's to be gained—the insights, the connection, the growth, rather than what's at stake—you foster an environment where emotions are less likely to derail constructive interaction. Positivity doesn't mean overlooking real issues or concerns; rather, it ensures you approach them with a mindset geared toward collaboration and resolution.

Incorporating these strategies in managing emotional responses isn't just beneficial for personal growth; it revolutionizes how we communicate on both personal and professional levels. As you hone these skills, observe their influence over your relationships. You may find that conflicts transform into dialogues of understanding and that strained relationships are forged into alliances of mutual respect.

As you continue on this journey of emotional intelligence in communication, remember that every interaction offers an opportunity to practice and refine these skills. Developing emotional agility not only equips you with the tools necessary to navigate any communicative landscape but ultimately cultivates deeper, more meaningful connections with those around you.

Chapter 9: Enhancing Communication in Teams

Effective team communication isn't just about exchanging information; it's the heartbeat of collaboration. Successful teams thrive on a dynamic interplay of open dialogue, active listening, and mutual respect, creating an environment where innovative ideas flourish and conflicts are swiftly navigated. Encouraging diverse viewpoints and fostering inclusivity are pivotal, as these elements ensure that every team member feels valued and heard. Implementing clear communication strategies can help dismantle silos, enhance productivity, and build strong collaborative bonds. By addressing potential barriers and emphasizing conflict resolution, teams can transform challenges into opportunities for growth. As we integrate these principles, the essence of team communication evolves from mere conversation to a powerful catalyst for achieving common goals.

Strategies for Effective Team Interaction

In today's dynamic workplaces, effective team interaction serves as more than just a functional necessity; it's a crucial element for cultivating innovation, engagement, and a thriving organizational culture. The art of team interaction is about more than just exchanging words. It's a complex dance of understanding, trust, and strategy that requires each member to play their part while attuning to the rhythms of others. This section delves into the essential strategies that teams can employ to enhance communication and maximize effectiveness.

First and foremost, establishing a foundation of trust within the team is critical. Trust doesn't happen overnight—it takes time and consistent behavior. Leaders and team members alike should prioritize transparency in interactions by openly sharing information, intentions, and even vulnerabilities. Consistent patterns of honesty and clarity not only build trust but also inspire an environment where team members feel safe to express their thoughts and ideas without fear of ridicule or retribution.

While trust sets the stage, a crucial element in effective team interaction is the role of active listening. Often, people listen only to respond, rather than to understand. Within a team, members should practice listening with the intent to comprehend fully. Reflective listening is a powerful tool here: by paraphrasing and repeating back what one has heard, team members demonstrate engagement and confirm understanding, minimizing the potential for miscommunication.

Another vital strategy is to create an inclusive communication environment. Encouraging diverse viewpoints not only enriches discussions but also stimulates creative problem-solving. Each team member should feel valued for their unique contributions. This can be achieved by actively seeking input from quieter members and recognizing that diverse perspectives can be instrumental in generating innovative solutions.

Acknowledging and managing emotions play a crucial role in team interactions. Emotional intelligence—understanding and managing one's emotions while being empathetic to the emotions of others—enables teams to navigate the interpersonal dynamics effectively. Teams that can identify emotional undercurrents and address them constructively can maintain harmony and focus on collaborative goals.

Regular and structured meetings serve as opportunities to align team goals and responsibilities while monitoring progress. However, meetings should be purposeful and efficient to avoid 'meeting fatigue.' Set a clear agenda, assign roles such as a facilitator and timekeeper, and encourage contributions while keeping discussions on track. This ensures that meetings are productive and foster a sense of accomplishment and direction among team members.

Feedback, when delivered thoughtfully, is a powerful catalyst for team development. Constructive feedback highlights areas for improvement and recognizes accomplishments, fueling motivation and growth. Teams should foster a feedback-rich culture where dialogue is continuous and bidirectional, focusing on behavior and impact rather than personal attributes.

Technology can serve as both an enabler and barrier in team interaction. While tools like collaborative platforms can enhance connectedness, they can also become a crutch that replaces meaningful face-to-face interactions. Teams should strive to balance digital communication with personal interaction, leveraging technology for convenience while preserving the human touch essential for building relationships.

Defining roles and responsibilities clearly can prevent confusion and overlap in tasks, ensuring smooth team operations. Role clarity empowers team members to take ownership of their tasks, knowing precisely how their contributions fit into the larger picture. This clarity promotes accountability, which, together with trust, underpins a high-functioning team dynamic.

A truly effective team interaction strategy includes provisions for handling conflicts constructively. Conflicts are inevitable but should not be avoided or suppressed. Instead, teams can adopt a mindset that views conflicts as opportunities for growth and innovation. Open dialogues that explore differing opinions can often lead to breakthroughs that passive agreement might never achieve.

Importantly, celebrating successes together reinforces cohesion and motivation. Whether achieved milestones are significant or seemingly insignificant, recognition fosters a sense of pride and belonging. Celebrations should be inclusive, ensuring all team members feel valued for their contributions, reinforcing their commitment to the collective mission.

Finally, continuous training in communication skills and team dynamics should be a priority. Investing in workshops or retreats that focus on building inter-personal skills can translate into tangible improvements in how teams interact and perform. These regular touchpoints are not only opportunities for skill-building but also for strengthening the camaraderie and unity of the team.

It's clear that effective team interaction requires a multifaceted approach. By weaving trust, active listening, emotional intelligence, and open communication into the fabric of team dynamics, teams can unlock their true potential. As organizations continue to evolve in complexity and interdependence, the skill of effective team interaction isn't just beneficial—it's imperative for success.

Resolving Team Conflicts

In the dynamic arena of team communication, conflicts are not only inevitable but also essential for growth. While they might initially appear as obstacles, they are, in essence, opportunities for deeper understanding and collaborative problem-solving. The challenge lies in managing these conflicts constructively without allowing them to derail the team's objectives. Disagreements can, without a doubt, serve as a catalyst for innovation and change if navigated wisely and with empathy.

Understanding the root of a conflict is the first critical step towards resolution. Team conflicts often stem from miscommunication, differences in values or goals, or the pressure of tight deadlines. Taking the time to understand underlying issues can prevent minor disagreements from escalating into major crises. This requires a level of introspection and openness to see conflict not as a personal attack but as a problem associated that needs a solution.

A common pitfall teams encounter is the tendency to avoid conflict altogether. This path of least resistance, however, rarely leads to harmonious outcomes. Suppressed tensions linger beneath the surface, resurfacing at inopportune moments and affecting team morale. Instead, addressing conflicts head-on with a solution-oriented mindset paves the way for genuine understanding and cohesion.

Effective conflict resolution requires a delicate balance of assertiveness and empathy. Assertiveness ensures that each team member's voice is heard and their concerns are addressed. When combined with empathy, assertiveness fosters an environment where everyone feels understood and valued. This two-pronged approach can dissolve hostility and build stronger alliances within the team.

At the heart of resolving any conflict is the ability to listen actively. Teams must cultivate an environment where listening is not just passive hearing but an active engagement with others' perspectives. When team members genuinely listen, they can comprehend issues from multiple angles, which helps in formulating balanced solutions. It's about surrendering pride and opening up to different viewpoints with an aim to integrate them into the final resolution.

Moreover, encouraging open communication helps in preventing conflicts. By setting a precedent where opinions are shared freely and respectfully, team members can air concerns before they fester into disputes. Open forums, where team members can express their thoughts without fear of retribution, create transparency and trust. Acknowledging feelings and validating emotions go a long way in showing team members that their contributions matter.

Resolution techniques such as compromise, collaboration, and consensus-building often prove effective in team conflicts. Compromise requires each party to make concessions, leading to a mutually acceptable outcome. While it doesn't always result in the best solution, compromise can be a practical way to quickly resolve lower-stakes issues. Collaboration, on the other hand, focuses on finding a win-win solution where the interests of all parties involved are integrated into the decision-making process. This approach is ideal for tackling complex and significant conflicts, though it requires more time and effort.

Instituting a process for conflict resolution within a team can also offer guidance in turbulent times. This process can include steps like establishing ground rules for respectful communication, identifying conflict themes, gathering everyone's input, and brainstorming solutions together. Clearly defined rules and processes empower individuals to resolve disputes efficiently and fairly, minimizing disruptions to team productivity.

It's crucial that teams foster a culture where mistakes and setbacks during conflict resolution aren't shunned but viewed as learning opportunities. If teams can reflect on what worked and what didn't, they can adapt more quickly to future challenges. This continuous learning process cultivates a resilient team capable of weathering conflicts with fortitude.

Leadership plays a pivotal role in setting the tone for conflict resolution. Leaders who exemplify calmness under pressure and demonstrate a willingness to engage in difficult conversations set a powerful example for their teams. Leaders should encourage openness by modeling the behaviors they wish to see in their teams—such as honesty, patience, and humility.

Lastly, teams should remember that developing effective conflict resolution skills is an ongoing journey that requires patience, practice, and a commitment to nurturing positive relationships. When conflicts are met with maturity and managed thoughtfully, they cease to be mere roadblocks and transform into stepping stones toward improved communication, stronger ties, and collective growth.

Chapter 10: Storytelling as a Communication Tool

As we delve into storytelling, we step into the heart of human connection. Storytelling isn't just an age-old tradition; it's a dynamic and powerful communication technique that bridges gaps, engages minds, and inspires action. A well-crafted narrative captures not just the imagination but also the emotions, allowing listeners to see through the storyteller's eyes and feel with their heart. This connection isn't merely circumstantial; it's rooted in our psychological makeup. Stories activate parts of our brain that allow us to transform the information into authentic experience, making it memorable and persuasive. Narratives compel us because they speak to our intrinsic need for meaning and understanding, transforming abstract ideas into relatable, tangible events. Whether you're persuading in boardrooms, lecturing in classrooms, or sharing with loved ones, storytelling can empower your communication, making your messages not only heard but felt. Harness this ancient tool's potential to not only convey information but to entertain, motivate, and build real, human connections.

Crafting Compelling Narratives

Amidst the bustling noise of modern communication, storytelling remains a timeless tool to captivate, inspire, and persuade. To understand why crafting compelling narratives is crucial, we need to delve into what makes stories so impactful. At its core, storytelling taps into our collective psyche, evoking emotions and memories in a way that pure facts and figures can't achieve. It's a dance between emotion and logic, weaving together imagery with intent to both engage the heart and enlighten the mind.

Consider the last story that moved you deeply. It likely didn't just state the protagonist's journey but painted it vividly, making you live through the highs and lows. The secret lies in relatability, where the listener sees a reflection of their own life experiences or aspirations within the story. A compelling narrative doesn't just tell; it shows and connects, fostering a sense of empathy. This connection is critical, especially in professional settings, where dry information can often fall flat.

To craft a compelling narrative, one must start with a clear understanding of the audience. What are their values, desires, and concerns? Tailoring a story to align with these elements ensures that the message hits home. It's not about shoehorning a preconceived idea into their lives but about integrating their reality into the narrative. This requires an astute observation and a willingness to adapt the story's framework to meet the audience where they stand.

Equally important is the structure of the story itself. A classic narrative arc comprises a beginning that sets the stage, a middle filled with conflict and trajectories, and a resonant conclusion. This structure is deeply embedded in our cognitive processing patterns, making it intuitive for audiences to follow. Yet, within this framework lies a wealth of creative freedom. Narratives don't have to be linear; they can loop, jump, and pivot, creating suspense and maintaining engagement.

The language of a narrative plays a vital role in its effectiveness. Words are power. Choosing vivid, illustrative language over bland statements transforms a story from mere recounting to an evocative experience. Metaphors, analogies, and imagery can significantly enhance understanding and retention, making abstract concepts tangible. However, it's essential to strike a balance—overly flowery language can overshadow the narrative, causing distraction rather than immersion.

Characters drive stories, just as much as plots do. Relatable characters allow the audience to project themselves into the narrative. They humanize complex topics and provide a lens through which the audience can view the circumstances presented. When crafting characters, it's imperative to lend them depth, giving them motivations, fallibilities, and an authentic voice that readers can recognize.

Tension and conflict are the essence of engaging storytelling. They generate anticipation, provoking thought and emotional investment. A story without challenges lacks the dynamic spark necessary to capture attention. The conflict doesn't need to be monumental to be effective. Even subtle, everyday struggles can resonate on a profound level when presented skillfully. It's the resolution of this tension, eventually, that often brings the most satisfaction, tying threads into a coherent tapestry.

Incorporating emotional appeal is another key aspect of a compelling narrative. Emotions compel us to act and make decisions more than logic alone ever could. A well-told story evokes feelings—be it joy, sadness, anger, or hope—triggering a deeper, more personal response. Effective storytellers know how to tap into these emotional reservoirs without coercion, gently guiding the narrative to inspire a genuine reaction.

Now, let's juxtaposition storytelling and persuasion. This relationship is at the heart of using narratives as communication tools. When a story aligns with an audience's values and beliefs, it naturally persuades without overt argumentation. It turns abstract ideologies into experiences that are tangible. Through identification with characters and scenarios depicted, audiences are coaxed into adopting new perspectives or reconsidering their current standpoints.

Feedback and refinement are essential in honing the craft of storytelling. Sharing one's narrative with diverse audiences can shed light on components that resonate or fall flat. Active listening to audience reactions can unveil nuances that might otherwise go unnoticed. As any experienced storyteller knows, the process is iterative and adaptive, always evolving to meet the needs and expectations of its recipients.

Animation through storytelling doesn't always necessitate grandiose tales of adventure. Sometimes, the most poignant narratives come from simplicity—stories of kindness, moments of change, or personal triumphs. These narratives, grounded in authenticity and truth, possess an unassuming power to connect on a human level. As much as flourishing imagination aids in storytelling, reality and authenticity anchor it in a relatable context.

The role of storytelling extends beyond mere communication; it envelops the realm of leadership, education, therapy, and positions of influence. Leaders use compelling narratives to galvanize teams and propel collective goals. Educators employ stories to embed complex lessons in memory. In therapy, personal narratives help to untangle emotions and perspectives, crafting paths towards healing.

In conclusion, when narratives are carefully and thoughtfully crafted, they become more than just stories. They become vessels of communication that transcend the mundane barriers that often blur understanding and hinder connection. The art of storytelling is dynamic, accessible, and ever relevant—a quintessential tool for those seeking to not only convey messages but to leave lasting imprints that provoke thought, catalyze change, and forge bonds. To master the craft is to hold a timeless key to effective and meaningful communication.

The Psychology of Storytelling

Storytelling is more than just a method of entertainment; it's a fundamental aspect of human communication that taps into our innate psychological processes. Our brains are wired to respond to stories in profound ways that go beyond the words themselves. When we tell a story, we're not merely conveying information. We're engaging in a deep-rooted tradition that shapes how we perceive, engage, and are persuaded by the world around us. Understanding the psychology behind storytelling can elevate our communication skills to new heights, enabling us to connect with others on both emotional and intellectual levels.

Stories have a unique power to captivate attention, a crucial component in effective communication. Our brains are evolutionarily geared to seek out patterns, and storytelling provides just that—a structured sequence that makes complex ideas more digestible. When information is presented in a narrative format, it gains coherence and predictability, which helps the listener or reader follow along with ease. This is why stories often succeed in maintaining engagement where dry statistics or isolated facts might fail.

At the heart of storytelling is its ability to evoke emotions and create empathy. Research has shown that listening to stories actually activates the same neural regions as those involved when experiencing events personally. Essentially, stories have the ability to transform listeners into participants, allowing them to live through the emotions and experiences of the protagonist. This emotional connection is a powerful tool for persuasion and influence. By harnessing the emotional appeal of storytelling, communicators can build rapport and genuine connection with their audience, which fosters trust and willingness to be influenced.

Another psychological component of storytelling is its capacity to enhance memory retention. Stories are often easier to remember than factual information alone. This is because stories often involve multiple elements such as character, setting, conflict, and resolution, which engage various cognitive faculties simultaneously. The structure of stories assists in organizing information in a manner that is more likely to be retained and recalled. Therefore, when complex information needs to be communicated and remembered, wrapping it in a narrative can significantly enhance its impact.

The communal nature of storytelling is another critical aspect. For millennia, humans have gathered around fires, in cave dwellings, and across tables to share tales that defined their cultures, societies, and individual identities. This social dimension of storytelling not only serves as a means of entertainment but also as a vehicle for communal learning and cohesion. By sharing stories, individuals can navigate shared experiences and values, cementing bonds and understanding within a community.

Moreover, storytelling has a unique way of bypassing resistance. When presented with facts and data, people often raise mental barriers as a defense mechanism. However, stories can sneak past these barriers by wrapping relevant information in a captivating narrative. This aspect of storytelling makes it an exemplary tool for overcoming skepticism and motivating change. By aligning a story's themes with the values and existing beliefs of your audience, you build a bridge that's not easily dismantled by doubt or disbelief.

Interestingly, storytelling also taps into the principle of causality. Humans have an inherent need to understand the cause and effect of events. Stories excel in satisfying this need by smoothly transitioning from one event to the next, providing explanations for actions and outcomes along the way. This seamless flow of information satisfies our curiosity and drives us to pay attention, always wondering what will happen next.

To be an effective storyteller, it's important to not only weave compelling narratives but to also understand your audience deeply. Tailoring your story to align with the listeners' experiences, values, and emotions is key to ensuring it resonates. This means asking questions before crafting your story: What do they value? What are their primary concerns or aspirations? By addressing these elements, you ensure that your story not only captures attention but is remembered and cherished.

But storytelling isn't just beneficial for the listener; it's also invaluable to the storyteller. Through the act of telling stories, individuals can process their own experiences, emotions, and beliefs. The very act of creating a narrative helps bring clarity and understanding to our own lives. It's a reflective process that allows us to see our past actions and emotions in a new light, promoting growth and self-awareness.

In professional settings, storytelling can be a game-changer. Whether you're leading a team, delivering a presentation, or negotiating a deal, framing your message in the context of a story can make your communication more effective. It brings a human element to the forefront, reminding your audience that at the end of the day, we're all driven by similar hopes, fears, and dreams.

Ultimately, the effectiveness of storytelling in communication boils down to its ability to connect at a deeply human level. By understanding and utilizing the psychology of storytelling, you can transform your interactions from mundane to memorable. In a world overflowing with information and complexity, the timeless power of storytelling provides a beacon of clarity and connection, encouraging others to listen, understand, and act.

Chapter 11: The Impact of Technology on Communication

As we delve into the evolving landscape of communication, we can't ignore the transformative role of technology. The digital era has radically reshaped how we connect, breaking geographical barriers and introducing new dynamics in our interactions. With tools like instant messaging and video conferencing, messages traverse the globe in seconds, yet the core principles of effective communication remain as vital as ever. It's crucial to navigate the deluge of digital platforms with purpose, ensuring that our communications remain authentic and impactful amid the noise. By harnessing technology wisely, we elevate our capacity to lead, persuade, and connect on a global scale. The key lies in balancing our tech-driven conveniences with the timeless essence of human connection, enabling us to communicate with clarity and empathy in an increasingly digital world.

Understanding Digital Communication

In today's rapidly changing world, digital communication has emerged as a fundamental pillar in how we connect, interact, and build relationships. It's not just about sending emails or instant messages; it's a transformative force that affects every facet of our communication. As technology evolves, so does our ability to convey messages across digital platforms, shaping perceptions in ways never before imagined. We are now more interconnected than at any other time in history, making it essential to grasp the nuances of digital communication to navigate this digital age confidently.

The digital landscape offers an abundance of platforms, each with its distinct features and user demographics. Social media, email, video conferencing tools, and instant messaging apps have become integral components of our daily lives. These platforms offer unprecedented opportunities to reach out and connect with diverse audiences. By understanding the strengths and limitations of these digital mediums, we can tailor our messages for maximum impact and effectiveness.

But digital communication isn't just about the platforms—it's about how we use them. Have you ever noticed the difference in tone when you read a message that's all caps versus one that's punctuated with emojis? The elements of digital communication, such as tonality, language choice, and multimedia usage, are crucial in conveying the intended message. These tools allow us to add emotional depth and clarity to our interactions, fostering better understanding and empathy among participants.

However, the paradox of digital communication is that while it can bridge vast distances, it can also create new forms of misunderstanding and disconnect. The absence of nonverbal cues like facial expressions, gestures, and tone of voice in text-based communication can lead to misinterpretations. This lack of context requires us to be more deliberate in our communication approach—choosing words carefully, considering our audience, and being mindful of the digital footprints we leave behind.

Consider how digital communication has transformed the workplace. Remote work, once a perk, has become a necessity for many. Organizations leverage digital platforms to maintain productivity and collaboration amongst dispersed teams. Video conferencing and collaboration tools, like Slack and Microsoft Teams, have replaced traditional face-to-face meetings, challenging us to adapt and hone our digital communication skills to ensure clarity and cohesion in team dynamics.

The influence of digital communication extends beyond professional settings. In our personal lives, social media platforms have revolutionized how we share milestones, opinions, and experiences with friends and family. But with these connections comes the challenge of authenticity. The curated nature of online personas and the pressure to present a certain image can sometimes lead to shallow interactions. Understanding the psychology behind social media interactions can guide us toward more genuine and meaningful digital relationships.

Moreover, the rise of artificial intelligence and chatbots in customer service and other industries further exemplifies the shift towards digital communication. These technologies streamline interactions and improve efficiency, yet they also redefine human roles in communication. Understanding how to interact with AI intelligently can enhance user experiences and ensure smoother communication flows in customer interactions.

The accessibility of digital communication brings an ethical dimension to the forefront. Privacy concerns, data security, and misinformation are pressing issues that demand vigilance and ethical considerations. Communicating responsibly in the digital realm is not just about adhering to legal standards but also about fostering trust and credibility with your audience. Creating an environment of transparency and respecting user privacy are foundational for maintaining integrity in digital communication.

As we immerse ourselves deeper into this digital landscape, it becomes clear that digital communication is an ever-evolving skill set. Embracing lifelong learning and adaptability will equip us to keep up with technological advancements and changing communication norms. Whether you're navigating remote work challenges or staying connected with loved ones across continents, developing a keen understanding of digital communication practices is key to thriving in our interconnected world.

Ultimately, the goal of mastering digital communication is to enhance our ability to connect with one another in meaningful ways—bridging gaps, fostering understanding, and building relationships that withstand the test of time and technology. By thoughtfully embracing these principles, we pave the way for more impactful and positive interactions in both our personal and professional lives.

Managing Communication Across Platforms

In today's world, communication is rarely confined to a single platform. We navigate through emails, chat apps, video calls, and social media, often within the same hour. Each platform possesses its own unique set of norms and expectations, complicating the landscape of effective communication. But mastering cross-platform communication isn't just about becoming tech-savvy; it's about understanding how to tailor your message to fit the medium while maintaining the core of what you want to say.

The first step in managing communication across platforms is understanding the strengths and limitations of each medium. For instance, emails are excellent for detailed, long-form communication and can serve as an official record. However, they lack the immediacy of instant messaging, which is better suited for quick exchanges. Video calls, on the other hand, offer a richness of interaction that includes nonverbal cues, which can enhance understanding but can be overwhelming and time-consuming for simple queries.

Choosing the right platform depends on your communication objective. If you want to foster a collaborative atmosphere, video calls or collaborative document platforms like Google Docs might be ideal. For managing tasks and deadlines, a project management tool like

Trello could be more effective. Understanding these distinctions helps you wield each tool where it's most potent, maximizing your efficiency and effectiveness.

When navigating these platforms, it's crucial to be deliberate about your tone and message structure. A casual tone on social media might be appropriate, while a more formal approach is often required in business emails. Knowing your audience on each platform and adjusting your communication accordingly can make a substantial difference. Asking yourself, "How do I want to be perceived?" can guide your tone choice, ensuring alignment with your communication goals.

Inevitably, with the proliferation of platforms comes increased potential for miscommunication. Emojis, once merely a whimsical addition, have become a critical tool for expressing tone and emotion, particularly in text-based communication where intention can be easily misconstrued. While they can add clarity, they also require preliminary understanding, which can vary among different cultures and generations—a smiley face might not always convey the same warmth to every recipient.

Equally significant is the strategic use of timing. The pace of online communication has quickened, injecting urgency into responses that might not require it. Recognizing when a delayed response is not only acceptable but beneficial is pivotal. Slowing down might give you the space to craft a more thoughtful and impactful message. This is especially relevant in professional contexts where immediate responses may inadvertently escalate pressure.

Transitioning between platforms fluidly requires both awareness and strategy. Context switching—jumping from one mode of communication to another—can hamper the quality of our messages. It's helpful to compartmentalize tasks and dedicate specific times to engage with different platforms. This structured approach minimizes cognitive load and enhances the quality of interactions.

The permanence of digital communication also adds another layer to consider. Written communications, particularly emails or public social media posts, may exist indefinitely. What seems appropriate today might be misaligned with tomorrow's norms. Understanding this can guide you in crafting messages that stand the test of time—considering potential future interpretations and impacts.

Additionally, don't underestimate the feedback loop created by digital communication. Platforms that allow for instant feedback, such as social media or chat apps, empower two-way communication and can foster a sense of community and collaboration. Embrace this feature strategically; positive interaction can reinforce strong communication skills and relationships, while constructive feedback can offer invaluable insights for improvement.

Moreover, technology offers tools to streamline communication management across platforms. Integrating apps that sync messages and updates can reduce the clutter of multiple channels. Recent advancements in AI also offer assistance, whether in scheduling or even crafting initial drafts of messages. Leveraging these technologies thoughtfully can enhance your communication strategy without sacrificing the personal touch.

While technology continues to evolve, so too must our communication strategies. Being adaptable and staying informed about new communication tools and platforms is essential. Continuously evaluating your communication strategy's effectiveness and making necessary adjustments ensures that your message remains both clear and impactful across any medium.

Ultimately, the aim is to create genuine connections regardless of platform. Understanding the nuances of each medium empowers you to connect authentically and purposefully, fostering relationships that are both meaningful and enduring. Mastering cross-platform communication not only broadens your reach but also deepens your connection with diverse audiences, a necessity in today's intertwined digital world.

Chapter 12: Handling Difficult Conversations

Every challenging conversation is an opportunity to deepen our understanding and connection with others. It's not just about voicing our thoughts but doing so with clarity, empathy, and purpose. When faced with difficult discussions, it's vital to approach them with a mindset of openness and collaboration, rather than confrontation or defensiveness. Embracing strategies such as active listening, emotional regulation, and empathy not only helps maintain composure but also transforms conflict into constructive dialogue. By focusing on shared goals and seeking mutual understanding, we enable ourselves to navigate these conversations confidently and with integrity, turning potential friction points into pathways for growth and improved relationships. As you engage in these dialogues, remember that every word and gesture can bridge gaps and build more resilient connections.

Strategies for Challenging Discussions

Challenging discussions are a part of everyday life, be it at work, home, or in social settings. The art of navigating these discussions lies in employing strategies that not only aid in resolving the conflicts at hand but also enhance personal and professional relationships. At the core of these strategies is an understanding of the psychological dynamics that accompany human interactions. By tapping into these dynamics, individuals can transform potentially contentious exchanges into productive dialogues.

One foundational strategy is preparation. Approaching a difficult conversation unprepared can lead to miscommunication and increased tension. Preparation involves understanding the context, the issues at stake, and the perspectives of all involved parties. Doing so allows you to anticipate possible reactions and counterarguments. Additionally, identifying your core objectives helps maintain focus and ensures that the conversation remains purposeful. This decrease in ambiguity often reduces anxiety for both parties, allowing for a more open and honest exchange.

Active listening is another critical component in handling challenging discussions. True listening goes beyond hearing words; it involves understanding the emotions and intentions behind them. By practicing empathetic listening, you can validate the speaker's feelings and demonstrate respect for their viewpoint. This validation often diffuses defensiveness and paves the way for finding common ground. Try echoing the speaker's sentiments—using phrases like "I hear what you're saying" or "I understand that this is important to you"—to show that you are genuinely engaged.

Equally important is the ability to manage one's emotions. Emotional intelligence plays a significant role in navigating difficult conversations. When emotions run high, logic often takes a backseat. Practicing self-awareness allows you to recognize your emotional triggers and manage your reactions effectively. Techniques such as taking deep breaths or pausing momentarily can help maintain composure, ensuring the conversation remains productive.

Language choice is another vital strategy. Using neutral and non-confrontational language can prevent further escalation of tensions. Words have power, and choosing them carefully can foster an atmosphere of collaboration rather than conflict. Avoiding accusatory phrases and adopting "I" statements, which focus on your feelings and experiences, can minimize defensiveness. For instance, saying "I feel overwhelmed when meetings run long" rather than "You always make meetings drag" shifts the focus from blame to a shared problem-solving approach.

Setting a positive tone from the onset can also influence the outcome of challenging discussions. By showing respect and maintaining a positive attitude, you set the stage for collaboration. Acknowledging the other person's contributions or perspective can build goodwill, which is crucial when navigating difficult topics. This doesn't mean you need to agree with everything, but recognizing the validity of their viewpoint can promote a more balanced dialogue.

It is also beneficial to establish ground rules before delving into a difficult conversation. These rules might include agreeing to take turns speaking, avoiding interruptions, or maintaining a respectful tone throughout. Setting such expectations helps create a controlled environment where both parties feel secure enough to express their thoughts freely. Moreover, agreeing on a time and place for the discussion, free from distractions, signals a shared commitment to resolving the issue at hand.

Moreover, embracing the power of pauses can effectively influence the trajectory of a difficult conversation. Strategic pauses give both parties time to process information and consider their responses carefully. It prevents the discussion from devolving into a rapid exchange of words with little understanding. Pauses demonstrate that you are taking the conversation seriously and reflecting on what's been said, which contributes to a more thoughtful dialogue.

In scenarios where consensus seems elusive, focusing on shared goals can serve as a unifying force. This involves identifying what both parties hope to achieve and directing the conversation toward these mutual objectives. Highlighting shared interests rather than differences can transform an adversarial exchange into a cooperative dialogue.

Working together towards a common goal fosters a team-like atmosphere and can result in more creative and effective solutions.

Understanding cultural and personality differences is also crucial in navigating challenging discussions. Being aware of different communication styles and adapting your approach accordingly can mitigate misunderstandings. For example, some individuals may prefer directness, while others might appreciate a more nuanced approach. Sensitivity to these differences fosters inclusivity and bridges the gap between varied perspectives.

Finally, humility and flexibility are indispensable attributes in challenging discussions. Recognizing that you don't have all the answers and being willing to alter your stance when presented with new, valid information demonstrates openness and fosters trust. Flexibility doesn't indicate weakness; rather, it showcases strength in adaptability and a commitment to growth and understanding.

In summary, mastering challenging discussions is a skill built on preparation, active listening, emotional regulation, and strategic communication. These strategies help transform difficult conversations into opportunities for connection and resolution, ultimately strengthening relationships and expanding understanding. By employing these techniques, you can navigate the complexities of human interaction with confidence and grace.

Maintaining Composure

Handling difficult conversations requires us to maintain composure, a skill that's vital yet often elusive. Composure acts as our anchor amidst the storms of challenging discussions, allowing us to navigate through them without losing sight of our goals or principles. Without it, emotions can escalate quickly, derailing the conversation and eroding trust. On the other hand, maintaining calmness can transform potential confrontations into productive exchanges. It becomes the baseline for crafting solutions and fostering mutual understanding.

The essence of composure lies in emotional intelligence, specifically in recognizing and regulating our emotions during intense interactions. This does not mean suppressing feelings or turning into an unemotional figure; rather, it's about observing emotions as they arise. When we're aware of our emotional state, we can choose how to respond instead of reacting impulsively. The practice of emotional regulation invites us to pause, breathe, and assess before speaking, all of which can prevent many unnecessary conflicts.

Consider a scenario at work where tensions might flare, such as receiving critical feedback from a superior. Instinctively, we might perceive this feedback as an attack, triggering defensiveness or even anger. However, maintaining composure means staying open and receptive, recognizing that this feedback is meant to encourage growth, not harm. By viewing the situation through a lens of optimism and understanding, we can respond constructively, asking questions and seeking clarity rather than reacting defensively.

Composure also involves managing our physical responses. Our bodies are tightly interwoven with our emotions. When anxiety kicks in, it's common for our heart rate to increase, palms to sweat, and muscles to tense up. These physical sensations can be overwhelming, clouding our judgment. Training ourselves to recognize these signs allows us to implement calming techniques, such as deep breathing or grounded awareness, to bring ourselves back to a state where we can think clearly.

Another crucial aspect of composure in difficult conversations is the art of balancing assertiveness with empathy. No conversation is truly productive if one simply bulldozes over the other participant's feelings and perspectives. Assertiveness means standing firm on our beliefs and expressing our thoughts clearly, without aggression or hostility. Coupling assertiveness with empathy—genuinely considering the other person's viewpoint—creates an environment where mutual respect flourishes and solutions are collaboratively reached.

This approach can be likened to a dance, where both parties move in tandem, guiding and responding in harmony to the rhythm of the conversation. It is within this dance that real understanding is born, as both parties contribute to and enrich the dialogue instead of vying for dominance or validation. The resulting synergy turns challenges into opportunities for connection and mutual growth.

Moreover, cultivating composure isn't something that happens overnight; it requires deliberate practice and reflection. Reflecting after conversations, especially those that were challenging, helps identify moments where composure was maintained or lost. Journaling thoughts and feelings about what worked well and what didn't can deepen our self-awareness and improve our future interactions. It's by analyzing our own strengths and shortcomings that we can develop a plan for building stronger composure in future conversations.

There are practical strategies one can adopt to enhance composure, such as the "stop, breathe, think, and respond" method. In practice, this technique encourages an individual to halt automatic reactions, take a few deep breaths to center themselves, contemplate the most beneficial response, and only then share their thoughts. Employing this strategy consistently can significantly alter the trajectory of a tense conversation, steering it towards a more thoughtful and grounded discourse.

In addition to individual techniques, the environment in which we communicate can also influence our composure. Identifying settings that make us feel secure and comfortable can help in maintaining calm. This might mean choosing a neutral ground for discussing contentious issues or setting a specific time when both parties can speak calmly and without external pressures. Environmental adjustments are subtle yet powerful cues that can aid in preserving calmness and focus.

Through these means, we not only see improvements in personal encounters but also professional ones, where stakes and pressures are often higher. Being the composed participant in a meeting can inspire confidence in colleagues and can often diffuse high-pressure situations simply by bringing an aura of calm and collectedness.

Ultimately, by nurturing composure, we are not only enhancing our communication skills but also fortifying relationships and fostering a collaborative spirit. Through conscious effort and practice, composure becomes the bedrock of difficult conversations, transforming them from barriers into bridges of deeper understanding and cooperation.

Chapter 13: Persuasion in Professional Settings

In the dynamic landscape of professional environments, persuasion emerges as a pivotal skill that can significantly impact career trajectories and workplace dynamics. Understanding the subtle art of persuasion in these settings isn't just about influencing others—it's about crafting win-win scenarios that foster collaboration and mutual respect. Effective persuasion requires a blend of strategic communication, emotional intelligence, and an acute awareness of both verbal and nonverbal cues. By mastering these elements, professionals can navigate complex workplace scenarios, align diverse perspectives, and catalyze career success. It's about striking a balance between assertiveness and empathy, ensuring that your message resonates while also respecting the viewpoints of others. This knowledge transforms professional interactions into opportunities for growth, reinforcing your reputation as a leader who can inspire and motivate. Whether it's securing buy-in for a project or navigating office politics, the ability to persuade judiciously can turn challenges into opportunities, paving the path for personal and organizational achievement.

Techniques for Career Success

In the realm of professional settings, persuasion isn't just an art—it's a critical skill that can be honed to achieve career success. The capacity to effectively persuade not only impacts the outcomes of individual interactions but also influences long-term career trajectories. Whether you're aiming for a promotion, looking to secure crucial resources, or trying to rally your team towards a common goal, mastering persuasion techniques can be pivotal.

First, let's start with understanding the audience. Knowing who you're trying to persuade is paramount. Are they data-driven or do they rely more on emotional storytelling? Tailoring your approach to the preferences and cognitive style of your audience can significantly increase your persuasive power. This involves doing your homework—learning about the background, values, and preferences of those you're trying to influence. By aligning your message with their values and concerns, you're more likely to capture their attention and agreement.

Another key to career success is establishing credibility, which can be achieved through consistent performance and integrity. People are more likely to be persuaded by someone they trust and respect. Demonstrating expertise in your field, being transparent in your communication, and following through on promises help build this crucial credibility. It acts as the bedrock upon which every persuasive message is built.

Being credible isn't enough. You must also be compelling and engaging. Storytelling is a powerful tool to create this engagement. In a corporate presentation or a team meeting, weaving facts and figures into a narrative can make them more relatable and memorable. Stories tap into emotions, making your audience more receptive to your message. Consider starting your next proposal by sharing a relevant anecdote that illustrates the potential impact of your ideas.

Moreover, active listening is a surprisingly persuasive tool. When colleagues feel heard and understood, they are more inclined to be open to your suggestions. It signals respect and validation, creating a collaborative rather than combative environment. Ask questions, seek clarifications, and provide affirmations to demonstrate your engagement and understanding. This turns persuasion into a two-way street, fostering mutual respect and cooperation.

Setting realistic goals and breaking them into attainable steps can also be a leverage point in persuasive communication. Proposing incremental improvements can often seem more feasible than sweeping changes, making others more willing to get on board. As your team or stakeholders see the tangible results from these smaller steps, they're likely to become more supportive of larger objectives.

It's also crucial to be adaptable. Workplace dynamics are ever-changing, and so are the ways in which people need to be persuaded. Flexibility in technique allows you to adjust to these changes. If one approach isn't effective, having the agility to pivot and try another can keep your persuasive efforts on track. This adaptability showcases your ability to respond to feedback and make necessary adjustments, which is a valuable quality in any professional setting.

Another important element is the strategic use of language. The words we choose can greatly affect how our message is received. Positive language tends to elicit positive responses. Avoiding negative or judgmental words helps maintain a respectful and open atmosphere, encouraging others to be more receptive to what you have to say. Pay attention to the tone and clarity of your message, as well. A clear, confident delivery can significantly reinforce your persuasion efforts.

Let's not forget about timing. Knowing when to propose an idea or request requires intuition and awareness of the surrounding circumstances. For example, approaching a manager about a new initiative when they're in the midst of a high-pressure project may not be ideal. Being patient and waiting for an opportune moment can enhance the likelihood of a favorable outcome.

Building alliance is another strategy for career success. Influencing decision-makers often involves garnering support from peers and team members. Having allies who endorse your ideas can create a ripple effect, prompting others to follow suit. This collective support can significantly amplify your persuasive ability.

In challenging situations, when persuasion seems tough, resilience and perseverance become your anchors. Understanding that rejection or pushback is part of the process can help you stay motivated. Analyze each setback to understand what worked, what didn't, and how you can improve in future attempts. This attitude not only helps you grow but also demonstrates your commitment and dedication to your colleagues and superiors, enhancing your standing in the workplace.

At the heart of successful persuasion lies a well-nurtured emotional intelligence. Being able to recognize and manage your own emotions, while simultaneously understanding and influencing the emotions of others, paves the way for effective persuasion. This skill helps you navigate complex interpersonal interactions and gain the cooperation of others.

Lastly, persuasion in professional settings is not just about winning arguments. It's about building and maintaining relationships. Base your persuasive strategies on genuine communication and mutual respect to foster an environment where influence is welcome and reciprocal. When others know that your aim is for the collective good rather than personal gain, they are more likely to align with your vision.

By employing these techniques, you can not only succeed in advancing your career but also become a valued and influential member of your professional community. The path to career success through persuasion involves continuous learning and adapting, but the rewards are immensely gratifying. It's about consistently cultivating your communication skills to effectively influence, inspire, and drive positive outcomes in your professional life.

Navigating Workplace Dynamics

In the professional arena, workplace dynamics wield a significant influence over the art of persuasion. Navigating these dynamics effectively is crucial not just for career advancement, but also for fostering a healthy work environment. At its core, workplace dynamics encapsulate interpersonal relationships, hierarchies, and the unwritten norms that govern behavior and communication within an organization. Whether you're in a leadership role or part of a team, understanding how to maneuver through these intricacies can make all the difference.

Consider the diverse nature of modern workplaces. They are melting pots of different personalities, backgrounds, and communication styles. Such diversity can be both a strength and a challenge. In persuading others, recognizing and adapting to individual differences is key. Some colleagues might be swayed by data-driven arguments, while others might respond better to storytelling or emotional appeal. The essence of successful persuasion lies in tailoring your approach to fit the audience, making your message resonate on a personal level.

Another aspect of workplace dynamics involves understanding organizational hierarchies and power structures. Each workplace has its own system of authority, which can shape communication flow. Knowing when to be assertive and when to show deference is a subtle art that, once mastered, can enhance your ability to persuade. It's not just about knowing who holds the title; it's about grasping who the key decision-makers are in a given context and aligning your strategies accordingly.

Interestingly, the informal networks—those uncharted channels of influence that often operate beneath formal structures—can hold remarkable sway. Identifying influential colleagues who might not hold high-ranking positions, yet command respect and have their ears finely tuned to the organizational pulse, can be pivotal. Establishing rapport with such individuals can aid in spreading ideas and gaining support, thereby enhancing your persuasive impact.

One must also navigate workplace politics with tact and diplomacy. Office politics, often perceived negatively, essentially revolve around relationships built on trust, reciprocity, and mutual benefit. Ignoring politics might seem noble, but doing so can inadvertently allow it to shape your reputation. Being politically savvy means understanding the dynamics at play without getting entangled in the web of manipulation. It's about managing perceptions while maintaining integrity.

Equally important is the climate of open communication fostered within a team. Organizations that encourage transparency and feedback tend to enjoy healthier dynamics, as team members feel valued and heard. As a persuasive communicator, leveraging this openness can amplify your effectiveness. Actively soliciting feedback, showing you value others' input, and being open to different perspectives not only enriches the communication process but also builds trust and credibility.

Conflict and its management are another integral part of workplace dynamics. Disagreements can disrupt harmony but can also be opportunities for growth and innovation if handled skillfully. Whether emotions run high or discussions remain cordial, mastering the art of resolving conflicts without diminishing relationships is a persuasive skill crucial in any professional setting. This involves listening actively, empathizing with opposing views, and negotiating solutions that all parties can accept.

Building emotional intelligence—tuning into your own emotions and those of others—is a transformative tool in navigating workplace dynamics. It enables you to discern nonverbal cues and empathize more deeply, enhancing your persuasive abilities. Colleagues who feel understood and supported are more likely to align with your ideas, fostering a cooperative environment.

Finally, adaptability remains a cornerstone of successful navigation through workplace dynamics. The only constant in today's work settings is change—be it through technological advancements, shifting market dynamics, or organizational restructuring. Being adaptable allows you to remain effective when strategies falter or context shifts. Approaching change with an open mind and a flexible strategy will enhance your persuasive ability and position you as a dependable and forward-thinking colleague or leader.

In conclusion, navigating workplace dynamics is a multifaceted endeavor that blends understanding of interpersonal relationships, organizational structures, and personal adaptability. By embracing the complexity of these dynamics, you can not only enhance your persuasive impact but also contribute to a thriving, harmonious work environment. As you refine your skills in this area, you'll find that persuasion becomes less about changing minds and more about connecting with people in meaningful ways. This connection fosters a genuine sense of collaboration and progress, underscoring the very essence of effective communication in professional settings.

Chapter 14: Communication in Leadership

Communication in leadership isn't just about delivering orders or managing tasks; it's about inspiring and motivating those around you to strive for excellence and embrace shared goals. True leadership communication requires the ability to convey a vision clearly, connect with others on an emotional level, and navigate challenges with confidence and integrity. By mastering the art of communicating with empathy and authenticity, leaders can foster a culture of trust and innovation. They know when to listen and when to speak, ensuring their messages resonate with diverse audiences. A leader's communication style sets the tone for an organization's culture, influencing motivation and productivity. By cultivating these essential skills, leaders not only guide their teams to success but also leave a lasting impact that transcends individual achievements, forging a legacy of positive influence and collective growth.

Developing Leadership Communication Skills

In the dynamic landscape of leadership, effective communication stands as a cornerstone of influence and success. A leader's ability to communicate with clarity and purpose not only impacts the morale and productivity of their team but also sets the tone for the organizational culture. To truly lead, one must cultivate a repertoire of communication skills that inspire and motivate, fostering an environment where ideas flourish and goals are achieved. Leadership communication isn't just about disseminating information; it's about crafting a vision, encouraging collaboration, and building trust.

At the heart of leadership communication is the art of listening. While speaking clearly and persuasively is crucial, listening actively can be even more transformative. Leaders who master active listening create a space where team members feel valued and heard, leading to higher engagement and innovation. When a leader genuinely listens, it isn't just about gathering information—it's about understanding the emotions and motivations behind the words. This empathetic approach not only strengthens relationships but also bridges gaps that might otherwise lead to misunderstandings or conflicts.

Equally important is the ability to tailor one's message to the audience. Whether addressing a team of seasoned professionals or a group of new hires, effective leaders adjust their communication style to meet the needs and preferences of their listeners. This requires a deep understanding of the audience's background, expectations, and concerns. By aligning the message with the listener's perspective, leaders can enhance their persuasiveness and ensure their communications resonate on a deeper level.

Consistency is another key attribute of effective leadership communication. Leaders who deliver consistent messages establish credibility and trust. When words and actions align, it reinforces the leader's reliability and integrity. This consistency also helps to reinforce organizational values and priorities, ensuring everyone is moving in the same direction. However, maintaining consistency requires vigilance and a keen awareness of one's communication patterns across different contexts and platforms.

Another vital aspect of developing leadership communication skills is the strategic use of storytelling. Stories captivate and engage, making complex ideas more relatable and memorable. Successful leaders weave stories into their communications to illustrate points, convey visions, and inspire action. A compelling narrative can provide clarity and direction, turning abstract concepts into tangible realities that people can connect with emotionally.

Moreover, inspirational communication isn't just about what is said but how it's said. A leader's body language, tone of voice, and even facial expressions play a significant role in conveying messages effectively. Leaders who display confidence and positivity through their nonverbal cues can enhance their verbal messages, making them more impactful. These elements can reinforce trust and reassurance, especially in times of uncertainty.

Leaders must also be adept at providing feedback—a crucial component of the communication loop. Constructive feedback, delivered in a way that's supportive and empowering, can lead to significant personal and professional growth for team members. By focusing on behaviors and outcomes rather than personal attributes, and by framing feedback within the context of growth and development, leaders can foster an environment that values continuous improvement.

In contrast, receiving feedback gracefully is equally important. By remaining open to criticism and viewing it as an opportunity for growth, leaders demonstrate humility and a commitment to personal development. This openness encourages a culture where feedback flows freely in all directions, contributing to an atmosphere of trust and respect.

Furthermore, adaptability is essential in the ever-evolving sphere of leadership communication. Leaders must be willing to revise their communication strategies in response to changing circumstances and technologies. Diversity of thought and open-mindedness are increasingly important as organizations become more multicultural and globally interconnected. Leaders who appreciate and leverage the unique perspectives of their diverse teams can create more inclusive and effective communication environments.

Lastly, it's crucial for leaders to cultivate their emotional intelligence. Recognizing and managing one's emotions while understanding the emotional states of others can drastically improve communication efficacy. Emotionally intelligent leaders can navigate conversations with empathy and tact, maintaining composure even in high-pressure situations, thereby encouraging the same resilience in their teams.

In conclusion, developing leadership communication skills is a multifaceted process that blends psychological insight with practical techniques. By focusing on active listening, message customization, consistency, storytelling, feedback, and emotional intelligence, leaders can enhance their influence and effectiveness. These skills not only help in achieving professional goals but also in building meaningful relationships that contribute to a thriving organizational culture. As leaders strive to communicate with intention and impact, they lay the groundwork for a legacy of positive influence and sustained success.

Inspiring and Motivating Others

In leadership, communication isn't just about getting your point across; it involves rallying people to a cause, energizing them, and unlocking their potential. Effective leaders can inspire and motivate others simply through the way they communicate. They harness the power of their words and actions to instill a sense of purpose and ignite passion. This demands more than a string of eloquent speeches or well-written memos—it's about connecting on a deeper level.

At the heart of inspiration lies authenticity. When leaders communicate authentically, they build trust. Authenticity breeds confidence because it presents a genuine portrayal of beliefs and values. Instead of hiding behind a facade, being transparent about intentions and reasons enables leaders to create a foundation of trust. Others are more willing to invest in a vision when they believe in the person behind it.

Consider the energy emanating from a passionate leader. Passion is infectious. It captivates attention and encourages others to take action. Imagine a leader who speaks with fervor about a mission, whose excitement is palpable. This kind of enthusiasm can transform a mundane task into a shared journey towards a meaningful goal. People are moved by emotion; by tapping into their emotional core, leaders can motivate teams to exceed expectations.

Yet, inspiring and motivating isn't about emotional highs alone. Leaders must also balance optimism with a grounded sense of reality. Acknowledging challenges openly, yet confidently steering the group through them, both builds credibility and keeps the collective spirit buoyed during difficult times. It's a delicate dance between acknowledging fears and reinforcing belief in the path forward.

Beyond verbal communication, leaders must model behaviors they wish to see. Actions often speak louder than words; consistent alignment of words and deeds reinforces motivational messages. A leader who values innovation must not only talk about its importance but actively engage in innovative practices. This congruence between talk and action solidifies leadership influence.

Moreover, effective leaders recognize the unique drive in each individual and tailor their approach accordingly. What motivates one person might not inspire another. Taking the time to understand personal aspirations and aligning them with organizational goals creates a sense of personal investment. This individual attention fosters a sense of belonging and importance within the team.

The art of storytelling is another powerful tool in a leader's motivational arsenal. Crafting a compelling narrative around a common objective can create a vivid image of the future that people can believe in. Stories resonate because they tap into universal human experiences. They make abstract goals tangible and create a shared vision that teams can rally around.

Effective communication in leadership also incorporates the strategic use of praise and recognition. Acknowledging achievements and expressing appreciation not only boosts morale but also reinforces desired behaviors. Celebrating even small victories contributes to a culture of positivity and encouragement, fueling continuous effort and dedication.

Leadership communication must also foster an environment where creativity and innovation can thrive. Encouraging open dialogue and valuing diverse perspectives spark inspiration. When people feel free to take risks and voice unconventional ideas, they are more likely to engage wholeheartedly. By actively listening to and valuing input from others, leaders can motivate teams through inclusivity and shared ownership.

Inspiring and motivating others hinges on a leader's capacity to communicate an engaging vision, embody the values they espouse, and cultivate an environment of trust and possibility. It's about weaving a narrative that binds people together for a greater purpose and guiding them through their own potential. By mastering these elements, leaders can truly inspire and motivate those around them to strive for collective success.

Chapter 15: Negotiation and Conflict Resolution

In the intricate dance of negotiation and conflict resolution, harnessing the power of effective communication becomes paramount. Not merely a transactional exchange, negotiation is a profound interplay of emotional intelligence and strategic thinking. When we approach conflicts with a mindset geared toward understanding rather than winning, we unlock pathways to creative solutions that benefit all parties involved. The art of negotiation is a balancing act—an exercise in listening actively, reading nonverbal cues, and fostering an environment where open dialogue thrives. In conflicts, understanding the underlying interests, and not just the positions, allows us to bridge gaps that seem insurmountable at first glance. By integrating empathy with assertiveness, individuals can navigate these challenging situations with grace, turning potential discord into opportunities for growth and collaborative success. Embrace negotiation not just as a means to an end, but as a journey of building stronger, more resilient connections through the power of well-crafted communication.

Strategies for Effective Negotiation

Negotiation is an art, a dance of words and intentions that brings together diverse interests and seeks a harmonious resolution. At its core, effective negotiation demands a blend of empathy, foresight, and strategic acumen. The first step is understanding that negotiation isn't about winning or losing—it's about finding a balance that honors all parties involved. While honing your negotiation strategies, it's crucial to adopt a mindset that embraces flexibility without forgoing your core objectives.

One of the key strategies is meticulous preparation. Before entering a negotiation, make sure you have a clear understanding of your goals and the possible outcomes. It's not just about knowing what you want, but understanding what the other party desires too. Gather information that allows you to anticipate their needs and concerns. This strategic insight forms the backbone of any negotiation, enabling you to craft proposals that are not only favorable to you but also palatable to the other side. Equipped with knowledge, you are less likely to be blindsided and more ready to adapt to the shifting dynamics of the negotiation table.

Building rapport is equally essential. This involves connecting on a human level, showing genuine interest, and creating a comfortable environment for dialogue. Reflective listening plays a pivotal role here—you need to show that you value the other person's perspective. Empathy doesn't mean you have to agree with everything; rather, it's about validating their feelings and thoughts. These efforts, seemingly peripheral, can significantly lower defenses and open pathways for more productive conversations.

Communicating clearly and effectively cannot be overstated. This means expressing your own needs and proposals in a manner that is straightforward yet tactful. Ambiguity can lead to misunderstandings, so aim to articulate your points with precision. Language is a powerful tool in negotiation. Employing positive language and avoiding aggressive tones can help maintain the flow of negotiation and keep both parties focused on reaching a resolution. Remember, words can inspire cooperation or sow discord—choose them wisely.

Another effective strategy is the use of the "principled negotiation" approach, popularized in various negotiation frameworks. This method emphasizes focusing on interests rather than positions. By aiming to uncover the fundamental needs and wants behind stated positions, negotiators can brainstorm multiple options that benefit all parties. A deeper understanding of underlying interests often reveals opportunities for creative problem-solving, transforming potential roadblocks into avenues of agreement.

In any negotiation, timing is critical. Knowing when to push forward or hold back your arguments can greatly influence the outcome. During discussions, pay attention to cues that signal a readiness to move forward or hesitation that may require more information or reassurance. Patience often becomes your greatest ally; rushing through segments can lead to overlooked details that might later prove significant.

It's also vital to have a negotiable range. Before stepping into discussions, define your best possible outcome (your goal) and your walk-away point. This flexibility allows you to engage confidently, knowing your limits while remaining open to compromise. Once these parameters are set, it becomes easier to navigate unexpected developments or stalemates with poise.

Negotiation also involves the delicate balance of assertiveness and accommodation. Assertiveness is about standing firm on your interests without being aggressive or dismissive. Accommodation, on the other hand, means being open to the other party's needs and adjusting your stance when necessary. Mastering this balance can enhance your credibility and influence, creating an atmosphere conducive to acceptable compromise.

A tactic often employed is the role of silence—an intentional pause can create space for reflection, allowing both parties to think and reevaluate. This can be especially effective after a proposal has been made or during moments of tension. Silence doesn't equate to agreement; it is a strategic pause that signals thoughtfulness and encourages the other party to fill the void, often leading to more voluntary disclosures or concessions.

Lastly, never underestimate the power of building a strong alternative to the negotiated agreement, commonly known as BATNA (Best Alternative to a Negotiated Agreement). By having a solid backup plan, you enhance your negotiating power and reduce the pressure of conceding to unfavorable terms. This knowledge empowers you, offering leverage to pursue your interests more assertively and strategically.

Integrating these negotiation strategies into your skillset takes practice and reflection. The most seasoned negotiators advocate for post-negotiation assessments—analyzing what went well, what didn't, and identifying areas for improvement. This cumulative knowledge fortifies your skills and enhances your ability to adapt to different negotiation contexts in the future.

In conclusion, effective negotiation is a symbiotic relationship between preparation and adaptability, empathy and assertiveness. By employing these strategies, you can transform the negotiation table from a battleground into a platform for collaboration and mutual understanding. As you hone your negotiation skills, you'll find yourself more equipped to navigate conflicts and pursue resolutions that are both effective and enduring.

Resolving Conflicts Peacefully

Conflict is an inevitable part of human interaction. It's not just a clash of opinions or interests but often an opportunity for growth, discovery, and stronger connections. The key is not in the conflict itself but in how it's resolved. Resolving conflicts peacefully is an art that can transform potential turmoil into productive dialogue. For anyone seeking to improve their communication skills, especially in navigating disagreements, adopting peaceful conflict resolution techniques is essential.

Understanding the underlying causes of conflict is the first step. Often, conflicts arise from unmet needs, miscommunications, or differing values. When we recognize these root causes, we're better equipped to address the issue at its core rather than just dealing with surface-level symptoms. Take the time to assess what each party genuinely needs and values in the conversation. By addressing these foundational elements, you can prevent the conflict from escalating.

Active listening plays a critical role in resolving conflicts. It's not just about hearing words but truly understanding the emotions and intentions behind them. When people feel heard, they're more open to compromise and finding common ground. Techniques such as reflecting back what you've heard, asking clarifying questions, and showing empathy can go a long way in calming tense situations. Show respect for the other party's perspective, even if you don't agree with it. This shows that you value their viewpoint, fostering an atmosphere of mutual respect.

Another powerful tool for peaceful conflict resolution is empathy. Empathy involves putting yourself in another person's shoes, imagining their feelings and experiences. It allows you to see the situation from their perspective, which can be a revelation. This understanding can not only bridge gaps but also cultivate patience and respect during heated exchanges. Express your empathy verbally by acknowledging their feelings, validating their experiences, and reassuring them of your sincere intent to resolve the issue amicably.

Effective communication is key to dissolving tension and preventing conflicts from spiraling out of control. This requires clarity, honesty, and assertiveness. You need to express your viewpoints confidently without aggression. Being clear about what you want and why it's important to you helps others understand your standpoint. More importantly, honesty builds trust—essential in any conflict resolution process. Always aim to convey messages without blame but with an intention to understand and be understood.

Acknowledging emotions during a conflict can seem counterintuitive, but it is critical. Emotions often drive conflicts, and ignoring them doesn't make them disappear. Acknowledging both your emotions and those of others humanizes the conflict. It reminds all parties involved that feelings are valid and need addressing. However, it's essential not to let emotions dictate actions. Maintain focus on resolving the issue rather than winning an argument.

Compromise is another vital aspect of resolving conflicts. It's not about one side conceding everything but finding a middle ground where both parties feel their needs are met. Effective compromise often involves negotiation and flexibility. It's about being open to alternatives and considering creative solutions that benefit everyone. By prioritizing the relationship over being 'right', compromises can strengthen bonds and improve future interactions.

Nonverbal communication also plays a significant role in conflict resolution. Actions often speak louder than words, and body language can either exacerbate or de-escalate a situation. Pay attention to cues such as eye contact, facial expressions, and posture—both your own and others'. They can provide invaluable insights into the emotional state of those involved. Adopting an open posture and maintaining calm, steady eye contact can convey sincerity and willingness to collaborate.

Setting the right environment can significantly impact the outcome of conflict resolution efforts. Aim for a neutral, relaxed setting where everyone feels comfortable to express themselves openly. This physical neutrality helps defuse tensions and sets the stage for productive discussions. It eliminates external pressures and distractions that can intensify the emotional stakes of the conflict.

Understanding cultural and individual differences can also enhance conflict resolution skills. Diverse perspectives bring rich dialogue, but they can also lead to misunderstandings without cultural awareness. Approach every conflict with an open mind, ready to respect and embrace varying viewpoints. This mindset not only helps in resolving current conflicts but also in fostering a more tolerant environment in the long term.

Practicing mindfulness can also be a transformative method in peaceful conflict resolution. Mindfulness helps you stay present, focused, and aware of your reactions. It allows for thoughtful responses instead of impulsive reactions. By practicing mindfulness, you develop better emotional regulation, preventing anger or frustration from clouding your judgment. This clarity and calmness are invaluable assets when handling heated discussions.

Finally, reflection post-conflict is an underrated but crucial step. Once a conflict is resolved, reflect on what went well and areas for improvement. This introspection provides insights into personal growth and enhances your conflict management skills over time. Consider questions like: What have I learned about myself? How can I communicate more effectively? This continuous improvement ensures that you're better prepared for future conflicts.

Peaceful conflict resolution is not a one-size-fits-all solution but a personalized approach. It's about knowing yourself, understanding others, and developing strategies that promote constructive dialogue. By adopting these techniques, not only can conflicts be resolved peacefully, but relationships can also emerge stronger and more resilient. Peaceful conflict resolution transforms adversities into opportunities, paving the way for better communication, collaboration, and understanding in all areas of life.

Chapter 16: Cultural Differences in Communication

In a world that's increasingly interconnected, understanding cultural differences in communication is essential for fostering meaningful interactions. Culture shapes how we interpret messages, express ourselves, and even perceive silence. Each culture has its unique set of norms, values, and communication styles that can deeply influence interpersonal exchanges. For instance, while Western cultures might prize directness and clarity, many Eastern cultures often value indirect communication and harmony. These differences can sometimes lead to misunderstandings or tensions if not navigated with sensitivity and awareness. To overcome these barriers, it's crucial to cultivate an open mind and a willingness to learn about others' backgrounds. This adaptability enhances your ability to connect authentically and effectively, paving the way for persuasion that's respectful and impactful across cultural boundaries. Embracing cultural diversity in communication isn't just about avoiding missteps—it's about appreciating the richness it brings to our interactions, enabling us to build stronger, more empathetic connections that transcend cultural lines.

Understanding Cross-Cultural Communication

In a world where globalization connects people from every corner of the earth, understanding cross-cultural communication has become more important than ever. Every culture possesses its own unique set of values, beliefs, and norms that inform how individuals communicate. These cultural underpinnings shape everything from language use and nonverbal signals to perception of time and space, directly impacting communication outcomes.

Consider the role of context in communication. In high-context cultures, such as those found in Japan and many Arab countries, people rely heavily on implicit messages and nonverbal cues. The meaning is often embedded in the context, and much is left unsaid. In stark contrast, low-context cultures like the United States and Germany place a stronger emphasis on explicit verbal communication, where clarity and directness are prized. This cultural divergence requires effective communicators to be highly adaptable, capable of shifting their approach depending on whom they're conversing with.

Misunderstandings often arise when communicators fail to recognize these fundamental differences. For instance, a seemingly innocuous gesture or phrase in one culture may be interpreted as offensive in another. It's not just about the words spoken but how they're interpreted through the cultural lens. This is where building cultural intelligence — the ability to relate and work effectively across cultures — becomes indispensable.

One might ask, how does one begin to develop cultural intelligence? It starts with awareness. Being conscious of one's own cultural biases and acknowledging the limitations of one's perspective is the first step toward meaningful cross-cultural interactions. This requires a shift from ethnocentrism, the tendency to view one's own culture as superior, to ethnorelativism, which appreciates the value of all cultures.

Active listening, a skill we've discussed in prior chapters, plays a crucial role in cross-cultural communication as well. When you listen intently, you not only hear the words but also perceive the nuances and emotions behind them. This depth of understanding fosters empathy, another cornerstone of effective cross-cultural exchanges. Empathy allows communicators to walk in others' shoes, gaining insight into their feelings and reactions, thus bridging cultural divides.

Furthermore, developing language skills beyond one's native tongue can serve as a powerful tool in cross-cultural communication. Language is not merely a vehicle for expressing thoughts — it reflects cultural values and priorities. Even a basic understanding of a second language can open up new channels of respect and rapport, breaking down the barriers set by linguistic differences.

Nonverbal communication, which we delved into in earlier chapters, also demands particular attention. Gestures, eye contact, and personal space vary significantly across cultures. For instance, while eye contact might signify confidence in Western cultures, it might be deemed disrespectful in some East Asian societies. An effective communicator must constantly calibrate these nonverbal cues, being mindful not only of their gestures but of interpreting others' as well.

Another critical aspect of cross-cultural communication is the difference in hierarchy perception. Power distance, a concept introduced by Dutch social psychologist Geert Hofstede, highlights how power is distributed within a culture. High power distance cultures accept a hierarchical order without much overlap between different social levels, which is often reflected in communication styles. Contrastingly, low power distance cultures advocate egalitarianism, which manifests in more informal and direct interactions. Navigating these nuances requires sensitivity and flexibility from communicators.

Time orientation also manifests in varied communication patterns among cultures. Cultures with a monochronic time system, often found in Western societies, prioritize punctuality and schedule adherence. Conversely, polychronic cultures, common in Latin America and the Middle East, view time more fluidly and place less emphasis on timely precision, focusing instead on relationships and interactions. Understanding these differences not only helps avoid conflicts but also enriches relationships with individuals from diverse backgrounds.

The exploration of cross-cultural communication extends beyond identifying differences; it's about embracing them to foster inclusivity and collaborative growth. To thrive in today's interconnected world, businesses, educational institutions, and individuals must cultivate a deep awareness of and respect for cultural diversity. As we learn to appreciate the richness that different cultures bring, we become more adept at crafting messages that resonate across cultural boundaries.

Undoubtedly, challenges persist in cross-cultural communication. Yet, by harnessing psychological insights and practical strategies, individuals can transform potential obstacles into opportunities for connection and understanding. As we've explored throughout this book, the key lies in an ongoing commitment to personal growth, empathy, and adaptability. By embracing these principles, communicators can truly understand and transcend cultural barriers, forging meaningful relationships that stand the test of time.

Overcoming Cultural Barriers

In our interconnected world, communicating across cultures isn't just a niche skill—it's a necessity. Yet, it's not without its challenges. Cultural barriers can create misunderstandings that impede clear communication. But these hurdles are not insurmountable. With thoughtful strategies and an open mind, you can bridge cultural divides and foster connections that transcend geographical borders.

First, let's talk about awareness. Before even attempting to communicate, one must develop an awareness of cultural differences. This isn't just about knowing that these differences exist; it's about understanding how deep they run. Culture influences not only how we express ourselves verbally but also how we interpret others' words, gestures, and intentions. By acknowledging these influences, we open ourselves to a world of understanding rather than misinterpretation.

A key step in overcoming cultural barriers is developing empathy. By putting ourselves in others' shoes, we can better appreciate their viewpoints and communication styles. Empathy allows you to see the world through different lenses, fostering patience and reducing the potential for conflict. Imagine sitting in a room where everyone's wearing different sunglasses. Recognizing that everyone views things differently is crucial for effective intercultural communication.

Listening actively is another powerful tool in your arsenal. When interacting with someone from another culture, listen more than you speak. This doesn't mean passivity; it means engagement. Ask questions, seek clarification, and take time to understand the context. Active listening not only builds rapport but also reduces misunderstandings, whether the topic is personal or professional.

Language barriers can be significant, but language also offers a bridge. Learning even a few phrases of a colleague's or client's native language can demonstrate respect and a willingness to connect. Of course, fluency isn't always achievable, nor necessary, but showing effort can speak volumes.

Nonverbal communication is often where cultural barriers become visible. Gestures, expressions, and even the use of personal space vary vastly between cultures. What might be a friendly gesture in one culture can be offensive in another. Therefore, it's essential to familiarize yourself with the nonverbal norms of different cultures. For instance, while direct eye contact is considered confidence in some Western cultures, it may be seen as disrespectful in certain Asian cultures. Understanding these nuances can prevent miscommunications before they happen.

Adaptability is the linchpin of overcoming cultural barriers. This means being open to changing your communication style to accommodate the other party. It could involve altering your speaking speed, modifying your tone, or choosing your words more carefully. Flexibility shows your commitment to effective communication and your respect for the other person's cultural background.

Be mindful of stereotypes. Stereotyping destroys genuine understanding and closes off possibilities for real connection. Instead of relying on these overgeneralizations, aim to understand individuals as they are. Remember that while cultural background influences behavior, it doesn't define every action or decision a person makes.

Seek cultural knowledge actively. Read literature, watch films, or engage with art from different cultures. These resources offer insights into the values, taboos, and humor unique to those cultures. Understanding these cultural products can provide context and depth to verbal communication, enriching interactions and reducing the likelihood of missteps.

Don't underestimate the power of technology in overcoming cultural barriers. Tools like translation apps and online language courses can support communication efforts significantly. Virtual meetings and collaborative software also make cross-cultural collaboration more feasible than ever. While technology isn't a substitute for genuine cultural understanding, it's an invaluable support tool in the global communication toolkit.

Feedback is invaluable. Encourage those you interact with to provide constructive criticism on your communication approach. This not only shows humility but also fosters an environment of continuous learning. It's through feedback that we refine our skills and better align them with cultural expectations.

Finally, patience is a virtue. Building effective cross-cultural communication isn't a one-time effort; it's a continuous process. Be patient with yourself and others as you navigate this complex terrain. Missteps are natural, but resilience and a commitment to improvement will lead to success.

Overcoming cultural barriers doesn't happen overnight, but with a mix of awareness, empathy, and adaptability, you can transform these challenges into opportunities for enriching and meaningful connections. The rewards of effective cross-cultural communication are immense—both personally and professionally—and well worth the effort.

Chapter 17: The Role of Feedback

Feedback isn't just a tool; it's the bridge connecting effort and improvement, communication and growth. In the art of communication, feedback acts as a mirror, reflecting not just what's working but also exposing areas ripe for enhancement. Giving feedback with empathy and receiving it with openness can transform our interactions, amplifying both understanding and influence. Skilled communicators harness feedback as a potent mechanism for evolution, encouraging honest dialogue that motivates and inspires. By cultivating an environment where feedback is both welcomed and valued, we ignite the spark of continuous learning and foster resilience in the face of challenges. This dynamic exchange turns the abstract into actionable guidance, nurturing potential and fostering authentic connections. Whether it's in a professional setting, a personal relationship, or even within oneself, feedback remains a critical compass in the journey of becoming a more effective and influential communicator.

Giving and Receiving Feedback

Feedback is one of the most powerful tools in communication, offering both the giver and the receiver a chance to grow, learn, and improve. At its core, feedback is about sharing information and perceptions that can help refine behaviors, enhance skills, and strengthen relationships. In both personal and professional realms, understanding how to effectively give and receive feedback can transform your interactions and open the door to deeper connections and more meaningful communication.

Giving feedback, when done correctly, is an act of care. It shows that you are invested in someone else's growth and success. But how do you deliver feedback that is constructive, well-received, and ultimately beneficial? Start with intention. Before offering your insights, consider your purpose. Are you aiming to guide improvement, recognize success, or simply share observations? Clarity in your intention helps frame your message constructively.

Consider the timing and setting of your feedback as well. A well-delivered message at an inappropriate time or place can lose its effectiveness. Choosing the right moment—when the other person is receptive and in a conducive environment—can significantly impact how your feedback is received. And remember, feedback is not a monologue. It's part of a dialogue, a conversation that allows for reactions and responses.

When you construct your message, be specific and clear. General feedback often fails to convey the necessary details that lead to improvement. If someone successfully executed a project, explain what exactly contributed to the success. Conversely, if someone's actions need improvement, identify the specific behaviors and their impacts. Unambiguous feedback helps avoid misunderstandings and fosters a productive dialogue.

Empathy plays a crucial role in providing feedback. Often, we approach feedback from our own perspective, forgetting to consider how the receiver might feel. Assume a mindset of empathy—how would you perceive the feedback if roles were reversed? Using "I" statements can soften the delivery and make it more about the shared situation rather than an individual's deficiencies. For example, say "I noticed that..." rather than "You did..."

On the flip side, receiving feedback can be challenging, even when given with the best intentions. Our instinct often propels us into defensive mode, eager to justify and explain. Master the art of listening actively and objectively. Pause before reacting, and consider the value of what is being said. Ensure you fully understand the message by asking clarifying questions, which shows your willingness to engage and improve.

Embracing a growth mindset is vital when receiving feedback. Instead of viewing feedback as criticism, see it as an opportunity for growth and learning. This shift in perspective can transform your experience, enabling you to harness feedback as a tool for developing your capabilities. Accept that everyone has areas to improve and that feedback is a stepping stone to achieving your personal and professional goals.

When receiving feedback, acknowledge the giver's perspective, even if it differs from your own view. Expressions of gratitude towards the person offering feedback can reinforce a positive cycle of communication. Let them know their insights are valued, which encourages an open and constructive communication environment. In this way, both parties can benefit—recognizing that feedback is a gift.

The art of feedback, both in giving and receiving, relies heavily on trust and respect. Trust enables open and honest communication, where feedback is viewed as a contribution, rather than a confrontation. Developing this trust takes time and effort—it's built on reliability, openness, and consistent, respectful interactions.

Receiving feedback graciously encourages others to continue this valuable exchange, fostering a culture of continuous improvement. It also models behavior for others. When individuals see feedback being handled well, they feel more motivated to offer and accept it themselves, strengthening the overall communicative environment.

Conversations around feedback don't happen in a vacuum; they exist within a broader context of relationships, goals, and shared experiences. They require maintenance. Follow-up conversations are beneficial to ascertain if changes have been noticed and to keep the feedback process dynamic and ongoing.

In conclusion, mastering the skills of giving and receiving feedback enhances your ability not only to communicate effectively but to influence and connect with others meaningfully. When approached with the right mindset and techniques, feedback becomes a catalyst for personal and collective growth, paving the way for more profound, more effective interactions.

Using Feedback for Growth

Feedback is an essential tool in communication, often serving as a mirror that reflects one's strengths and areas for improvement. However, it's not just about receiving feedback but using it wisely to spur personal and professional growth. In the world of communication, feedback creates a ripple effect, enhancing self-awareness and catalyzing development.

The willingness to accept feedback sets the groundwork for improvement. It requires a mindset that sees feedback not as criticism but as a guide for development. This distinction is crucial; without an open mind, the potential growth from feedback remains untapped. All effective communicators embrace a spirit of continuous learning. They understand that every piece of feedback is a key to unlocking new levels of understanding and skill in communication.

Understanding the emotions behind responses to feedback is vital. Often, when feedback touches tender spots, the initial reaction might be defensive. It's human nature. Yet, by recognizing and managing these emotional responses, one can transition from resistance to acceptance. This shift allows an individual to view feedback as constructive rather than critical. Embracing emotional intelligence in these moments opens the door to immense personal growth.

Practical application of feedback is where true growth occurs. It's one thing to hear feedback and another to act on it. Setting clear, actionable goals based on feedback helps bridge the gap between theory and practice. Whether it's tweaking presentation skills or honing active listening, taking small, measurable steps forward ensures that feedback translates into progress.

Peer feedback offers a unique perspective that can be invaluable for personal development. Often, peers can provide insights that might be overlooked by oneself. They witness one's communication style firsthand and can identify both strengths and areas needing improvement. It's essential to create an environment where peers feel comfortable sharing their observations openly and honestly. This feedback loop not only enhances individual growth but can also strengthen team dynamics.

Consider the importance of feedback for self-reflection. Reflecting on the feedback received allows for deeper insights to emerge. Through reflection, one can identify patterns and trends in communication habits. This understanding paves the way for more targeted development, ensuring efforts are directed where they are most needed. Journaling about feedback experiences can be a powerful tool, helping to track progress and maintain motivation.

Feedback should also be balanced and unbiased. When providing feedback to others, it's crucial to ensure that the insights offered are constructive and aimed at fostering growth. Equally, when receiving feedback, evaluating its fairness and considering its source is essential. External opinions may sometimes be skewed by personal biases or misunderstandings. By remaining objective, one can distill valuable lessons from the feedback that truly matter.

Finally, gratitude plays a significant role in using feedback for growth. Being thankful for feedback, regardless of its nature, fosters a positive cycle of improvement. It demonstrates respect and openness to continuous learning. Expressing gratitude encourages a culture of sharing and receiving feedback within teams and communities, enhancing communication effectiveness for everyone involved.

In summary, feedback is the compass that guides communicators on their journey of growth. Through openness, reflection, and action, feedback transforms from mere words into profound learning opportunities. It's the key that unlocks potential, fueling improvement and fostering a culture of ongoing development in the realm of communication. By embracing the power of feedback, one doesn't just grow individually but contributes to the collective advancement of effective communication skills.

Chapter 18: Developing Confidence in Communication

Building confidence in communication begins with understanding the interplay between self-belief and expressive clarity. It's not just about speaking; it's about conveying your ideas with conviction, even when doubt looms. Imagine entering a conversation with a sense of assurance that your perspective holds value—this mindset changes everything. Rather than succumbing to self-doubt, embrace opportunities to express yourself, knowing that each interaction is a step toward enhancing your communication prowess. By focusing on your strengths and experiences, you can nurture a confident voice that both informs and inspires. This journey is about more than mastering verbal skills; it's about creating genuine connections that resonate. So, push past hesitations, embrace your unique viewpoint, and let your confidence propel your communication to new heights.

Building Self-Confidence

Building self-confidence isn't just about speaking up; it's about believing that your voice matters. It's knowing that your contributions can make a difference, not just professionally but personally. Confidence in communication is a process, a combination of self-awareness, practice, and the willingness to face discomforts that come with stepping out of your comfort zone.

One crucial step to building self-confidence is understanding the power of self-perception. How you view yourself directly influences how others perceive you. Consider this: a person who believes they deserve to be heard will communicate with conviction and clarity. Start by identifying personal strengths and openly acknowledging them. This self-reflection isn't an exercise in arrogance but a foundation for authentic confidence.

Practice is another essential element in gaining confidence. Like any other skill, communication improves with use. And practicing in varied settings—whether casual conversations or formal presentations—can significantly enhance your comfort level. With every interaction, you'll notice incremental gains in assurance. This goes a long way in reducing anxiety, allowing you to remain more present and engaged.

Feedback plays a significant role in developing self-confidence. Constructive criticism, when viewed as an opportunity rather than a threat, can catalyze improvement. Engaging with feedback requires not only listening but also the resilience to incorporate changes and the understanding that growth is not linear. Balanced feedback fosters a mindset that embraces mistakes as learning experiences.

Visualization is a powerful technique often used by skilled communicators. Picture yourself succeeding in communication scenarios, whether it's acing a presentation or having a meaningful conversation. Visualization primes your mind for success and builds a familiar path for positive outcomes. This mental rehearsal reduces anxiety, helping you handle real situations with greater poise and self-assurance.

Communication confidence is also strengthened by setting small, achievable goals. Instead of aspiring to be perfectly eloquent overnight, focus on making a single point clearly in each interaction. Or decide to speak up at least once during a meeting. Small wins accumulate, gradually reshaping your self-efficacy. As your confidence grows, so will the scope of your goals.

Understanding and embracing your communication style can be liberating. Not everyone needs to be a silver-tongued orator. Whether you're naturally assertive or more contemplative, honoring your authentic voice is key. This authenticity not only boosts your confidence but also makes your communication more genuine and relatable.

Body language is another critical factor in building communication confidence. How you physically present yourself can alter your mindset. Simple acts like standing up straight, maintaining eye contact, and using open gestures can not only make you seem more confident but can actually make you feel it. These outward signs of confidence can create a positive feedback loop, reinforcing your inner sense of assurance.

The language you use when speaking to yourself internally can also affect your self-confidence. Positive self-talk, replacing self-doubt with encouraging affirmations, is pivotal. When you catch yourself thinking negatively about your communication abilities, shift your perspective to focus on what you've achieved and what you're capable of achieving. This mental shift can transform your entire approach to interactions.

Notably, confidence is closely linked to preparation. Being well-prepared for communication events minimizes the unknown and allows you to present information with authority. Whether it's knowing your material inside out for a presentation or having a clear intention for a conversation, preparation sets the stage for success and reduces apprehension.

It's vital to remember that building self-confidence in communication is a journey, marked by progress, not perfection. It's about showing up, being present, and valuing your contributions. Trust in your capability to learn and adapt, and over time, effective communication will become not only a skill but a source of personal empowerment.

Overcoming Self-Doubt

Self-doubt can feel like a shadow that follows you every time you open your mouth to speak or convey an idea. It whispers uncertainties and possible failures, often influencing your ability to communicate confidently. But like any shadow, it diminishes when you shine a light on its source. Overcoming self-doubt is less about eradicating fear and more about understanding it, reframing it, and ultimately using it to fuel your journey toward confidence in communication.

One of the first steps in overcoming self-doubt is recognizing its presence. Self-doubt often masquerades as 'realistic thinking' or 'self-protection,' but its true nature is rooted in fear—fear of judgment, rejection, or failure. A certain level of doubt is normal and can even be healthy, acting as a checkpoint for humility and growth. However, when it becomes a significant hindrance, undermining your communication efforts, it's time to address it head-on.

Understanding the origin of your self-doubt can be a transformative experience. It might stem from past experiences where communication didn't go as planned, harsh feedback, or deeply ingrained beliefs imposed by others. By shining a light on these origins, you begin to dismantle their control over you. Reflection and introspection allow you to see these doubts not as insurmountable barriers, but as obstacles you can navigate around.

A powerful technique to combat self-doubt is reframing your internal dialogue. The words we use in self-reflection shape our perceptions and capabilities. If your internal dialogue is peppered with phrases like "I'm not good enough" or "I always fail at this," then that's the narrative you're weaving into your communication attempts. Instead, adopt a narrative that acknowledges challenges but emphasizes growth and learning. Words hold power; leverage them to build yourself up rather than tear yourself down.

Gradually, practice stepping out of your comfort zone. Begin with familiar or low-stakes scenarios to build your confidence. You might find comfort in crafting a script or outline for what you wish to communicate. Such preparations anchor you, helping you stay focused on your main message, while providing a safe space to experiment with varying levels of assertiveness and self-expression. As you notice small wins, these victories accumulate, gradually eroding the foundations of your self-doubt.

Another valuable approach is seeking feedback from trusted sources. Honest feedback, when delivered constructively, becomes a mirror reflecting not only areas for improvement but also highlighting your strengths. When you start acknowledging and embracing positive feedback, you challenge the narratives driven by self-doubt. Positive reinforcement from others can sometimes illuminate strengths you might find yourself blind to.

Meditation and mindfulness can also play a significant role. By nurturing a mindful approach to your thoughts, you develop the ability to catch self-doubt early in its tracks, disconnecting from it as an irrefutable truth. Mindfulness helps you view these thoughts as transient reflections rather than concrete facts. This separation is crucial in maintaining a sense of perspective, allowing you to choose how much power you give your doubts.

Importantly, don't shy away from vulnerability; it can be a powerful ally. When you open yourself to the possibility of being wrong or not having all the answers, it paradoxically strengthens your position. Vulnerability invites connection, endears you to your audience, and projects authenticity, which is a cornerstone of effective communication. Embracing vulnerability reduces the fear of making mistakes, as you start viewing them as essential parts of the communication tapestry rather than catastrophic failures.

It's also crucial to cultivate a strong sense of purpose in your communication endeavors. When your message or conversation is driven by a clear purpose or passion, it minimizes the focus on doubts and redirects energy toward achieving the broader objective. Purpose anchors you, providing a counterbalance to self-doubt, as your commitment to the message overshadows the fears tied to execution or reception.

Consider developing the practice of visualizing success. Visualizations can prepare your mind for positive outcomes, countering negativity with imagery of successful interactions. This mental rehearsal programs your psyche with expectations of positive experiences, thus gradually reinforcing your confidence in real-world situations. Visualization becomes a powerful antidote to the debilitating effects of lingering self-doubt.

As you reflect on these practices, remember that overcoming self-doubt is a journey rather than a destination. It requires patience and kindness toward oneself, recognizing that setbacks are not failures but steps in the learning process. Each foe of self-doubt surmounted extracts lessons that add to your resilience, subtly extending your comfort zones in communication.

Ultimately, developing confidence in communication hinges not on the absence of self-doubt, but on the courage to proceed in its presence. The path might be fraught with hesitations, but each stride forward echoes louder than the doubts that pursued you at its onset. Communicating effectively is less about being flawless and more about being authentically you, fear and all. Every step you take in facing your doubts marks a victory in your pursuit of confident, impactful communication.

Chapter 19: Mindful Communication

In the fast-paced world of constant distractions and digital overload, "mindful communication" emerges as a powerful remedy for fostering genuine connections. It's not just about hearing words but truly understanding the intent and emotion behind them. By practicing mindfulness in conversations, we cultivate an awareness that allows us to be present, attentive, and empathetic. This heightened presence transforms interactions, encouraging us to respond with intention rather than react impulsively. When we're mindful, we create a space where both parties feel respected and valued, making it easier to navigate misunderstandings and build trust. Through this artful blend of mindfulness and communication, we enhance our ability to impact others positively, creating more meaningful and fulfilling interactions.

Practicing Mindfulness in Conversations

Mindful communication transcends mere words exchanged between people; it's about infusing every dialogue with awareness and presence. Imagine a conversation where each word, gesture, and silence is an opportunity for deep connection. That's the essence of practicing mindfulness in communication—being fully present with our thoughts, feelings, and intentions while engaging with others.

One of the core tenets of mindfulness in conversations is active awareness. This means not only hearing the words spoken but also attuning oneself to the emotional undertones and the nonverbal signals that accompany them. Many of us fall into the trap of thinking about our response while the other person is still talking. To practice mindfulness, we need to consciously stop our mind's chatter and truly listen with the intention of understanding before responding.

Consider the idea of "listening with your whole body." This involves using not just our ears but also our eyes and intuition to fully grasp what the speaker is conveying. When we maintain eye contact, nod in understanding, or provide nonverbal feedback, we communicate that we're engaged. This type of presence can't be faked; it must be genuine to foster trust and understanding.

Mindful conversations are not only about listening but also about responding thoughtfully. It's about recognizing the space between stimulus and response—the brief moment where we choose our words and tone. This practice allows us to consider the impact of our responses, ensuring they're in alignment with our values and the context of the discussion.

Stress and emotional reactivity are common barriers to mindful communication. When emotions run high, it's easy to react impulsively. Practicing mindfulness involves acknowledging these emotions without being ruled by them. Taking a deep breath, pausing, and reflecting before speaking can help in crafting responses that are both considerate and effective.

While mindfulness can enhance any type of conversation, it is particularly beneficial during difficult discussions. Here, the stakes are high, and miscommunication can lead to conflict or misunderstanding. Mindfulness helps us to keep our emotions in check, listen with empathy, and communicate our thoughts clearly, reducing the likelihood of exacerbating tension.

Moreover, mindful communication fosters higher levels of empathy and compassion. When we're fully present, we become more attuned to the experiences and perspectives of those we engage with. This deep understanding enhances the connection and often leads to more harmonious interactions.

Incorporating mindfulness into our conversational practice can also improve our ability to negotiate and influence. When others feel seen and heard, they're more likely to be open to our viewpoints and suggestions. Mindfulness facilitates this by creating an environment of openness and mutual respect.

Another benefit of mindful conversations is the enhancement of personal relationships. By being present, attentive, and sincere, we cultivate a sense of trust and intimacy. People appreciate when they're given undivided attention and when their perspectives are valued, which strengthens bonds over time.

Practicing mindfulness in conversations is not something that happens overnight; it's a skill that requires continuous practice and reflection. Begin by setting an intention to be mindful before engaging in any conversation. You might find it helpful to take a few moments to center yourself and focus on your breath to clear your mind.

In practice, this could mean turning off distractions, such as mobile devices, to focus solely on the person you're communicating with. It could also involve reflecting on past conversations to identify moments where mindfulness was lacking and considering how you can bring more awareness into future interactions.

Mindfulness in conversations also extends to the way we speak. Being mindful of our language involves choosing our words carefully and being aware of the tone and pace of our speech. It's about ensuring that our words are aligned with our true intentions and are crafted to encourage understanding rather than division.

While practicing mindfulness in communication can be challenging, particularly in the fast-paced world we live in, remember that it's about progress, not perfection. Each conversation is an opportunity to practice, refine, and grow. Embrace the journey and notice how each mindful interaction enriches your connections and your communication prowess.

Ultimately, as we cultivate mindfulness in our conversations, we contribute to a more compassionate and understanding world. The ripple effects of mindful communication extend beyond individual interactions to influence communities and cultures, creating a foundation for more meaningful and effective engagement.

Benefits of Being Present

In a world full of distractions, being present in a conversation is often overlooked but immensely powerful. How often have we found ourselves planning our response while the other person is speaking or fiddling with our phones during a seemingly mundane chat? The habit of being mentally absent while physically present not only diminishes the quality of our interactions but also erodes our ability to forge genuine connections. Being present, really present, involves much more than just hearing words; it demands that we tune into the emotional undertones, the pauses, and even the gestures that accompany speech.

Being present can transform a mundane exchange into a meaningful dialogue. When we fully engage, we don't just listen with our ears but also with our entire being—our attentiveness radiates through our body language, facial expressions, and even the silence we hold with reverence during the conversation. This level of engagement sends a clear message: "I value what you have to say." This is an essential component of mindful communication.

Moreover, when we're present in conversation, we open the doors to deeper empathy and understanding. By unfolding the layers of what's said and unsaid, we recognize the needs and emotions of others.

This empathetic engagement enables us to respond more genuinely and effectively, reducing conflicts and misconceptions. Presence aids in creating space for both parties to voice their feelings, leading to more fulfilling and cooperative interactions.

The practice of presence also fosters a greater level of authenticity. Our responses become less about rehearsed reactions and more about spontaneous, real-time reflections of our thoughts and feelings. This authenticity paves the way for stronger trust and credibility—a cornerstone of any meaningful relationship. In a corporate setting, it can make the difference between a leader who is respected and one who is merely obeyed.

In this state of presence, time seems to slow down, allowing us to savor the richness of human connection. It grants us the patience to let someone else take the conversational floor, encouraging a more balanced exchange instead of a battle for dialogue dominance. This creates a more harmonious rhythm in relationships, both personal and professional, where both parties feel heard and acknowledged.

Presence isn't just beneficial for the person we're communicating with; it enhances our own experience too. By focusing fully on the present moment, we mitigate the effects of stress and anxiety that often stem from mulling over past events or worrying about the future. Being present helps us to handle interactions more creatively and flexibly, responding to real-time reactions rather than preconceived notions.

In the realm of decision-making and problem-solving, presence reframes our understanding. It enables us to take in diverse perspectives without bias, encouraging out-of-the-box solutions that might otherwise be overlooked. This heightened awareness contributes to more equitable outcomes, both in negotiations and in resolving conflicts, fostering satisfaction and goodwill over time.

Furthermore, being present enhances our ability to influence effectively. When people sense that we are truly engaged, their natural inclination is to reciprocate. This mutual engagement creates a conducive environment for persuasion, where ideas can flow and take root more comfortably. Constant focus and engagement can also weatherproof relationships, equipping them to withstand disagreements because the underlying trust remains unshaken.

There's a richness in being present that's akin to savoring a well-prepared meal—relishing every ingredient, decoding each flavor, and appreciating the artistry. In many ways, conversations are no different when approached with mindfulness. The benefits of being present aren't merely psychological or emotional; they extend into professional realms, enriching our capabilities as leaders, colleagues, and mentors.

On a personal level, the art of being present nurtures our overall sense of well-being. It grounds us, anchoring our minds in positivity and reality. By embracing the current moment wholeheartedly, we can shed regrets and future anticipations, living more fulfilling and balanced lives. For those seeking personal development, honing the skill of presence is transformative—enabling them to navigate the complexities of human interaction with grace and efficacy.

Mindful communication powered by presence is an eloquent dance of attention and intention. It invites us into a dynamic tableau where we're not mere participants but architects of meaningful, impactful communication. In recognizing the power of being present, we tap into a timeless truth: that the quality of our interactions often defines the quality of our lives.

Chapter 20: Communication for Personal Development

As we explore the nuances of communication for personal development, it's important to recognize how central our interactions are in shaping our personal journeys. Communication isn't just about exchanging words; it's a powerful tool that can be harnessed to achieve personal goals and enrich our relationships. When we communicate with intention and clarity, we set the stage for personal growth and self-discovery. Here's where the magic happens: by engaging in honest dialogue, asking the right questions, and genuinely listening, we foster an environment that enhances trust and understanding, ultimately deepening the connections we cherish. True personal development invites us to not only express ourselves more authentically but also to inspire others to do the same, creating a ripple effect of positive transformation. This symbiotic relationship between communication and personal growth reflects the undeniable impact of human interaction in realizing our potential and cultivating meaningful relationships.

Using Communication to Achieve Personal Goals

Communication isn't just about exchanging information; it's a tool capable of transforming personal ambitions into reality. Unlocking the true potential of your communication skills helps you articulate your goals clearly, surmount barriers, and foster relationships that propel you towards your objectives. In the competitive landscape of personal growth, being able to eloquently express your aspirations can set the stage for success. A blend of assertive expression and empathetic listening can be a powerful combination, enabling you to navigate towards your personal goals with confidence and precision.

At the heart of using communication for personal development is the ability to persuade and influence. Whether it's negotiating a raise at work, rallying support for a personal project, or simply convincing yourself of your own capabilities, persuasive communication is indispensable. To wield this power effectively, it's essential to understand the psychological underpinnings of influence. People are naturally inclined to respond positively to those they trust and understand. Hence, building rapport through genuine interactions is crucial. Being congruent in your verbal and nonverbal signals and consistently demonstrating sincerity can foster a robust foundation of trust.

On this journey, it's paramount to not only communicate outwardly but to engage in meaningful self-dialogue as well. The way you talk to yourself matters. If your internal dialogue is plagued with self-doubt or negativity, it becomes a roadblock to achieving your personal objectives. Conversely, nurturing a positive inner conversation can boost self-confidence and endurance. It's about reprogramming your thoughts with constructive affirmations that align with your goals, creating an internal environment that supports growth and achievement.

It's equally important to customize your communication style according to your audience. This requires an understanding of the diverse personalities and preferences you might encounter. For instance, while some may prefer direct and concise messages, others appreciate a more narrative approach. Adapting your delivery not only ensures that your message is received but also endears you to diverse audiences, expanding your sphere of influence. Effective communicators are like chameleons, adjusting their strategies to suit different contexts and individuals without losing their authenticity.

Moreover, setting clear, communicable goals is vital. Instead of vaguely wishing for success, specify what you seek to achieve. This clarity helps you convey your intentions with precision, whether you're discussing them with a mentor, a partner, or a peer. The specificity of your goals enhances their salience in communications, encouraging others to rally around you and provide support or resources that might be essential to your journey. In this sense, communication acts not just as a means to convey your goals but as a catalyst that mobilizes the necessary elements around them.

Achieving personal milestones is often a collaborative effort, which makes relationship-building an integral part of the process. People are inherently social beings, and cultivating networks based on mutual benefits can accelerate your progress. It's about understanding the give-and-take dynamic—offering value to others while also being open to receiving help. Maintaining an open line of communication with your network ensures a free flow of ideas, feedback, and opportunities. By engaging actively and sincerely with your network, you create allies who might be instrumental in propelling you toward your personal aspirations.

In navigating personal relationships, active listening emerges as a key communication skill. Listening is more than allowing another person to talk; it's about understanding their perspective and responding empathetically. When you listen actively, you foster an environment of trust and openness. This doesn't only benefit your relationships; it also enriches your own understanding, potentially unveiling new goals or pathways you hadn't considered. It's about being present and fully engaged in conversations, which can lead to more meaningful interactions and outcomes.

Conflicts, whether internal or external, are inevitable on the path to personal development. Having strategies to resolve these conflicts is essential. Clear and assertive communication can aid in this process, defusing misunderstandings before they escalate. Open dialogues aimed at understanding the root causes of conflicts often reveal insights that can help adjust your strategies or goals. Embracing conflict as a chance to grow and refine your communication skills can be transformative, shifting perspectives and fostering resilience in the face of challenges.

Technology has also reshaped how we use communication to achieve personal goals. Digital platforms offer new ways to connect, share, and influence, but they require a nuanced approach. Online communication lacks the nuance of face-to-face interaction, making it essential to be more deliberate in crafting messages. Ensuring clarity and warmth in your digital correspondence can maintain and even enhance the connections you have, aligning them more closely with your aims. Being adept at digital communication can open up new avenues for achieving personal aspirations that transcend geographical limitations.

Ultimately, using communication to achieve personal goals is about alignment and congruence. It's ensuring that what you say, how you say it, and the actions you take are all in harmony with your personal mission. This alignment not only propels you toward your goals but also ensures integrity and authenticity in your interactions. It's about harnessing the full spectrum of your communication skills, from articulating your vision with clarity to listening deeply and responding with empathy.

By mastering these elements, you not only move closer to your personal goals but also enrich your journey with deeper connections and insights. In the end, every word spoken, every interaction you have, becomes a stepping stone towards the fulfillment of your personal ambitions. Communication, when leveraged skillfully, becomes the bridge between where you are and where you aspire to be.

Enhancing Personal Relationships

Effective communication serves as the backbone for any meaningful relationship. It's more than just exchanging words; it's about forging connections that enrich our lives and the lives of others. While we often focus on communication in professional settings or public speaking, enhancing personal relationships through communication is equally critical. To develop strong, lasting personal bonds, we must look beyond words and delve into the subtleties of connection, which encompass understanding, empathy, and shared experiences.

Empathy transforms ordinary exchanges into significant relationships. By genuinely listening and expressing a sincere understanding of another's feelings, we open the pathways to deeper connections. This doesn't merely involve waiting for our turn to speak but actively engaging with the other person's experiences, feelings, and thoughts. When someone feels heard, they feel valued. By implementing empathy in our daily interactions, we can foster intimacy and trust that withstands the test of time.

Moreover, patience plays an integral role in communication for personal development. It's crucial to understand that everyone has a unique pace and style of communication. By practicing patience, we allow others the breathing room to express themselves fully without the pressure of immediate judgment or interruption. Patience allows us to better navigate the nuances of human emotion, leading to healthier and more productive discussions.

One can't overlook the importance of nonverbal cues in enhancing personal relationships. Body language, facial expressions, and even the tone of voice we use contribute significantly to how our message is received. A simple smile or a nod can add layers of meaning that words alone may not convey. Being aware of and responsive to these nonverbal signals can enrich our communications, providing a fuller understanding of the emotions and intentions at play.

While verbal and nonverbal cues form the foundation of effective communication, maintaining a balanced give-and-take dynamic within conversations can't be overstated. Successful relationships aren't one-sided; they require both parties to actively contribute and receive. This balance prevents feelings of neglect or dominance, promoting a sense of shared space where both individuals can express themselves freely and authentically.

Conflicts, though inevitable in any relationship, can also be opportunities for growth and connection if handled with care and understanding. Rather than avoiding difficult topics, embracing them with a mindset geared towards resolution can strengthen the ties between people. Approaching conflicts with an open mind and a focus on constructive dialogue leads to new insights and deeper appreciation of each other's perspectives.

Shared experiences significantly impact the quality of personal relationships. Participating actively in moments together, whether joyous or challenging, creates a sense of unity and shared purpose. These experiences often become the bedrock of memories that individuals cherish and rely upon during tough times, hence reinforcing the relationship's depth and resilience.

Another key element is acknowledgment and appreciation. Recognizing the efforts and contributions of those we care about fortifies the bond and builds a mutual respect. Simple expressions of gratitude for little things can have a profound impact. They act as reminders of one's value in the dynamic, fostering a positive and nurturing environment.

Regular reflection on how we communicate within our personal relationships can lead to continual improvement. By stepping back and assessing our interactions, we identify areas where we might be inadvertently closing off communication or failing to recognize the needs of others. This introspection can inspire personal growth and elevate the quality of our connections.

Technology often influences how we communicate today, offering both opportunities and challenges. While digital communication can keep us connected, it's essential to balance it with face-to-face interactions where possible. Emphasizing personal presence over digital presence helps maintain the richness and depth that personal relationships require.

Finally, humor and positivity can't be underestimated. Bringing light-heartedness into conversations can ease tensions and add joy, making interactions more pleasant and memorable. Humor can bridge gaps and connect people in unexpected ways, reinforcing bonds with laughter and shared delight.

In conclusion, enhancing personal relationships through communication is a multifaceted effort that requires intentionality, empathy, and a willingness to engage deeply with others. By focusing on these aspects, we lay the groundwork for personal development that resonates with the very core of human connection, leading to more fulfilling and enduring relationships.

Chapter 21: The Future of Communication

As we stand at the precipice of tomorrow, the evolving landscape of communication presents both challenges and breathtaking opportunities. New technologies, from augmented reality to AI-driven platforms, are reshaping how we engage with each other, breaking down barriers of distance and time. In the hustle of these digital innovations, it's crucial to retain the essence of human connection—empathy and understanding. The future demands not just adaptability but an intentional focus on cultivating authentic interactions, whether through virtual meetings or global collaborations. Preparing for this tectonic shift means embracing a mindset where psychological principles guide our use of these tools, ensuring that technology enhances rather than hinders our ability to build genuine relationships. By staying informed about these trends and honing our skills to navigate them, we can wield the power of communication to inspire, influence, and connect with people worldwide, ensuring that our voices resonate soundly in whatever form the future brings.

Trends and Innovations

As we plunge into the future of communication, it's clear that we're on the cusp of dramatic changes. The confluence of advanced technologies and evolving social dynamics is reshaping how we connect, inform, and influence. This transformation is not just technological; it's profoundly psychological, affecting the very essence of our interactions.

Among the most groundbreaking trends is the increasing integration of artificial intelligence (AI) in communication. AI's ability to process vast amounts of data allows it to discern patterns and provide insights that humans alone might struggle to uncover. This capability is revolutionizing how we understand and react to conversations, both personal and professional. Imagine AI-assisted tools that help us tweak our messaging in real-time to better resonate with our audience or chatbots that can handle customer queries with emotional intelligence, detecting frustration or satisfaction purely from text. These innovations are propelling us into a realm where machines understand us more intuitively.

Additionally, virtual and augmented reality (VR/AR) are making headway, transforming workplaces, educational environments, and social interactions. The immersive experiences offered by these platforms allow for richer and more engaging communication. They offer new ways to convey emotions and intentions that static images or plain text cannot. For example, in a virtual meeting, the subtlety of a nod or the nuance of tone can be conveyed almost as effectively as it would be in person. The psychological impact of such immersive interactions can lead to deeper understanding and stronger connections.

This leads us to the rise of remote communication tools, a trend undeniably accelerated by recent global events. As hybrid and remote work become the norm, we're witnessing an innovation surge in tools designed to make virtual communication as seamless as face-to-face interaction. Platforms are adopting features to keep participants engaged, such as breakout rooms and instant polling, while also incorporating AI to monitor engagement and suggest ways to enhance it. The psychology of remote work communication involves understanding how to maintain human connection without physical presence, a challenge that technology is increasingly addressing.

Another fascinating development is the personalization of communication experiences. As big data becomes more prevalent, so too does our ability to personalize communication strategies. Businesses can tailor their messages down to the individual level, understanding what resonates best with each demographic or even each person. This hyper-personalization is creating more meaningful dialogues and strengthening brand loyalty by appealing directly to the needs and emotions of individuals.

Social media platforms are continually evolving, influencing how we communicate on a large scale. The power of social media lies in its immediacy and reach, but its evolution now focuses on creating spaces for richer and healthier interactions. New features aimed at encouraging positive engagement, reducing misinformation, and promoting mental well-being are becoming standard. This shift reflects a broader societal need to foster more meaningful connections in digital spaces.

Moreover, the increasing importance of transparency and authenticity cannot be overlooked. In an age where information is abundant but trust is scarce, the demand for honest and transparent communication is rising. This trend is seen in the expectation that organizations, leaders, and influencers communicate openly about their values and decisions. Authentic communication builds trust and credibility, cornerstones of successful relationships both online and offline.

Focusing more on the workplace, communication software is evolving to ensure inclusivity and accessibility. With more diverse teams, the tools we use must accommodate different languages, cultural contexts, and accessibility needs. Innovations here include real-time language translation, transcription services, and assistive technologies for those with disabilities. Such advancements are critical for fostering an inclusive environment where everyone can contribute meaningfully.

Finally, as technology advances, it's easy to overlook the importance of the human element in communication. While these innovations offer exciting possibilities, they also pose challenges that must be harmonized with human-centric approaches. We must remember that technology's role is to supplement and enhance—not replace—the empathetic, perceptive abilities that define human connection. While technology provides the tools, it's ultimately the user who determines how successfully these tools are leveraged.

The future of communication is undoubtedly promising, with trends and innovations that hold the potential to solve some of the most pressing challenges in how we connect and collaborate. Embracing these changes requires an adaptability to the technologies that are redefining the landscape, as well as an understanding of the psychological principles that continue to underpin effective communication. By striking a balance between innovation and authenticity, we can ensure a future where communication not only evolves but flourishes.

Preparing for Future Challenges

As we navigate the rapidly shifting landscape of communication, preparing for future challenges becomes not just valuable but essential. The evolution of communication is marked by a pace that's faster than ever, fueled by technological advancements and shifting cultural landscapes. Embracing change is not only about keeping up; it's about proactively preparing for what's next. In this context, honing psychological strategies that can withstand and adapt to these changes is crucial. By doing so, we can ensure meaningful, effective communication in any scenario, no matter how unforeseen.

One significant aspect of preparing for future communication challenges involves understanding the intersection of technology and human interaction. While technology can streamline and enhance our communications, it also introduces new complexities. Ensuring that these tools serve us rather than hinder us requires a deep understanding of their psychological impact. Balancing virtual and in-person interactions is a skill that will only grow in importance as we advance further into the digital age.

Moreover, as global connectivity increases, the ability to navigate multicultural communication becomes critical. Cultural sensitivity and awareness are paramount when communicating across diverse populations. Understanding the nuances in nonverbal cues, verbal expressions, and communication styles across cultures will equip us to connect genuinely and respectfully.

Preparing for these challenges also involves anticipating shifts in social norms and values. As societies evolve, so do the expectations around communication. What's considered appropriate or effective can change rapidly, highlighting the importance of staying informed and adaptable. This awareness allows us to craft messages that resonate and build rapport in varying contexts, safeguarding our communications against becoming outdated or ineffective.

Another key area is emotional intelligence, which remains a steadfast pillar in effective communication regardless of changes around us. Its relevance is reaffirmed as we confront future challenges—understanding and managing emotions in ourselves and others is crucial, especially against the backdrop of rapid technological and societal shifts. The ability to remain empathetic and emotionally aware transcends temporal changes and ensures our communication remains grounded and human.

To anticipate future challenges, we must also focus on developing resilience in our communication strategies. Resilience allows individuals and organizations to bounce back from setbacks and thrive despite obstacles. In communication, this means being able to adapt messages, strategies, and methods to continue achieving our intended impact, even under adverse circumstances.

Additionally, fostering an environment of continuous learning and growth is vital. As communication paradigms shift, being open to new ideas, technologies, and methodologies will keep us prepared. Encouraging curiosity and innovation within teams and networks ensures that adaptability becomes a built-in mechanism rather than a reactionary measure.

The rise of artificial intelligence and machine learning in communication tools presents both opportunities and challenges. Leveraging AI for efficiency and precision can enhance our communicative efforts, yet it requires a cautious approach to ensure human elements are not lost. Communicators will need to maintain the delicate balance between leveraging technology and retaining the authenticity of human connection.

In preparing for the future, developing critical thinking skills becomes indispensable. Analyzing and interpreting information critically allows us to navigate through the increasing volume and complexity of data we encounter. In communication, this means discerning valuable insights from noise and crafting coherent messages that convey truth and build trust.

As we steer through these preparations, we must consciously include the ethical implications of our communication strategies. The future presents new ethical dilemmas, with privacy, misinformation, and accessibility at the forefront. Navigating these challenges requires a commitment to integrity and the ability to foster transparent, inclusive communication practices.

Lastly, preparing for future communication challenges means embracing adaptability as a core skill. In an environment marked by continuous change, flexibility becomes our strongest asset. By cultivating a mindset open to learning and adapting, we position ourselves to handle any curveball communication might throw our way.

In conclusion, the future of communication is rich with challenges and opportunities. By preparing strategically, staying informed, and fostering resilience, we equip ourselves to meet these challenges head-on. Our ability to connect, influence, and communicate effectively relies not on predicting the future, but on our readiness to embrace and adapt to its unfolding landscape.

Chapter 22: Using Humor and Positivity

In the intricate dance of communication, humor and positivity emerge as potent partners, wielding the ability to transcend barriers and foster genuine connections. When we infuse our interactions with laughter, we don't just lighten the mood; we create an inviting atmosphere where open engagement becomes possible. Humor has the magical prowess to break down defenses, turning skepticism into receptivity. It acts as a bridge that draws people closer, making them more amenable to our ideas. Positivity complements this by fueling conversations with enthusiasm and warmth, which in turn boosts morale and encourages collaboration. Together, humor and positivity transform ordinary exchanges into memorable experiences, reinforcing bonds and unlocking doors to new opportunities. Embracing these elements not only enhances our ability to persuade but also enriches our relationships, creating a ripple effect that encourages others to respond in kind.

Benefits of Humor in Communication

Humor in communication is like the invisible thread that can bind people together. It's a powerful tool that can disarm conflict, put a smile on a stranger's face, and create an atmosphere of warmth and connection. At its core, humor has a unique way of transforming serious moments into lighter, more approachable dialogues. This transformation often leads to open and genuine interactions, which build trust and strengthen relationships.

A key benefit of using humor is its ability to act as a social lubricant. It eases conversations, making them less awkward and more engaging. In groups where tension might deter open dialogue, a well-timed joke or humorous observation can break the ice, setting the stage for more meaningful exchanges. The ability to laugh together is often viewed as a shared human experience, bridging gaps between individuals and fostering a sense of unity.

Moreover, humor can enhance message retention. When a message is delivered humorously, it becomes more memorable. Imagine two presentations: one filled with dry facts and another peppered with clever anecdotes—more often than not, the latter will stick longer in the audience's mind. This is due to the emotional resonance that humor evokes, anchoring information in the brain more effectively.

Humor also boosts approachability and likeability. A leader or colleague who demonstrates a good sense of humor is often perceived as more approachable and relatable. This can diminish feelings of intimidation or hierarchy, encouraging colleagues to express ideas and concerns without fear. In professional settings, this cultivates a culture where individual voices are heard, and contributions are valued.

At the psychological level, laughter triggers the release of endorphins, the body's natural feel-good chemicals. This physiological response not only reduces stress but can also improve overall mood and perspective. When people feel good, they are more open to collaborative problem-solving and creative thinking. It's as if humor unlocks parts of the brain that foster adaptive and flexible thought processes.

In conflict situations, humor can serve as a tactical tool. It helps de-escalate tension and can redirect the focus from issues to solutions. A touch of humor demonstrates that the person remains optimistic and solutions-oriented, even in challenging scenarios. This optimistic approach often inspires others to adopt a similar perspective, reducing defensiveness and opening up avenues for reconciliation.

Furthermore, humor can act as a catalyst for innovation. In environments that nurture creativity, humor provides a safe space for unconventional thinking. It allows individuals to play with ideas freely, without self-editing due to fear of judgment. The resulting imaginative atmospheres are conducive to breakthrough innovations and inventive solutions to complex problems.

However, it's crucial to wield humor with sensitivity and awareness. What is funny to one person can be offensive to another. Hence, effective communicators are attuned to their audience's cultural and personal boundaries, ensuring that humor is used inclusively and respectfully. Recognizing the context and adjusting the tone accordingly ensures that humor remains a bridge rather than a barrier in communication.

Another dimension worth exploring is the therapeutic potential of humor. When dealing with difficult emotions or topics, humor can offer a reprieve, allowing for reflection without overwhelming negativity. It creates a safe zone where issues can be aired without colliding head-on with emotional walls. By lightening the moment, humor can facilitate a more open exploration of thoughts and feelings, paving the way for healing and understanding.

In educational settings, humor can serve as an invaluable teaching aid. Educators who employ humor effectively can increase student engagement and participation. By making lessons entertaining, students can foster a deeper connection with the material, resulting in better comprehension and retention. It's the classic case of learning through laughter.

In conclusion, humor in communication is not merely an entertainment tool but a powerful enhancer that strengthens interpersonal connections, enhances retention, and breeds creativity. It helps alleviate stress, resolve conflicts, and build bridges across diverse groups. By appreciating the nuance humor requires, communicators can wield it adeptly to nurture positive, productive, and meaningful interactions. It's a delightful art that, when mastered, enriches the tapestry of human communication.

Creating Positive Interactions

Humor and positivity aren't just nice add-ons to our conversations; they're essential tools in fostering effective and meaningful communication. Creating positive interactions enables us to connect on deeper emotional levels, opening pathways to understanding and agreement that might otherwise remain closed. When we inject humor and positivity into our interactions, we're not just speaking; we're engaging in a dance of mutual respect and shared humanity.

At the heart of creating positive interactions is the principle of approachability. Humor can act as a social lubricant, breaking down barriers that often impede open communication. By lightening the mood, it not only helps draw others in but also eases tension in potentially charged situations. A shared laugh can turn a difficult conversation into a collaborative one, removing defenses and bridging divides.

Yet, humor isn't one-size-fits-all. It's crucial to tailor your humor to your audience. What may be hilarious to one person might be off-putting to another. Understanding the context and the shared experiences of those you're communicating with ensures your humor resonates and fosters inclusivity rather than alienation. In this way, humor becomes a tool of connection, aligned with empathy and understanding.

Positivity, much like humor, serves as a counterbalance to stress and negativity that often pervade our interactions. A positive approach can redefine the outcome of a discussion, infusing it with hope and possibility. This doesn't mean ignoring challenges or glossing over real issues; rather, it's about framing our conversations in a way that highlights possibilities instead of impossibilities. By being consciously positive, we inspire and motivate action, encouraging others to engage with a mindset of potential and growth.

An important aspect of fostering positive interactions is recognizing the impact of our words and actions. Words are powerful—they have the ability to uplift or deflate, to build or break. When we choose our words carefully, we can inspire a similar level of thoughtfulness in others, setting the stage for interactions that are constructive and affirming. Even in disagreement, a positive tone can remind us of our shared goals and help maintain mutual respect.

Moreover, expressing gratitude and appreciation is an impactful way to cultivate positivity within interactions. A simple "thank you" or acknowledgment of someone's effort can transform the dynamic of any relationship. It demonstrates recognition and value, which fosters mutual respect and, more importantly, encourages further positive behavior. When people feel valued, they're more inclined to contribute and invest in the interaction positively.

Nonverbal cues also play a significant role in communicating positivity. A genuine smile, for instance, is universally understood and can have an immediate impact on how others perceive you. It presents warmth and openness, qualities that naturally invite positive engagement. Similarly, maintaining open and enthusiastic body language signals receptivity and willingness to engage, essential elements in creating positive interactions.

Despite all these strategies, creating consistently positive interactions requires authenticity and consistency. People are quick to spot inauthenticity, and a lack of genuineness can undermine your efforts. Ensure that your positivity is rooted in sincerity and that humor isn't forced. Being genuine is crucial and can result in more meaningful and lasting connections.

Active listening, too, enriches our positive interactions. By truly listening, we're validating others' experiences, signaling that their thoughts and feelings matter. This validation builds a foundation of trust and respect, essential for any positive interaction. It also opens up opportunities for more honest and fruitful conversations, where everyone involved feels heard and respected.

Additionally, cultivating a mindset of curiosity can significantly impact the quality of your interactions. Approaching conversations with the intent to learn rather than to teach or persuade invites openness. This curiosity not only enriches the dialogue but also allows us to see things from perspectives we might not have considered. A curious mindset fosters a willingness to understand, which can be the seed from which positive interactions grow.

The ability to adapt is yet another ingredient for successful interactions. Situations and dynamics can change rapidly, and being flexible in your approach to communication can help maintain positivity. Whether it's altering your conversational style to suit the mood or adjusting your humor to fit the social setting, adaptability suggests a level of empathy and consideration for others, strengthening the quality of your interactions.

In summary, creating positive interactions through humor and positivity isn't about painting an unrealistically rosy picture of the world. It's about recognizing the inherent value in every interaction and choosing to make it as constructive and rewarding as possible. Whether you're making someone laugh or infusing a conversation with a hopeful perspective, these strategies serve not only to enhance the immediate communication but to foster long-term connections built on mutual growth and understanding.

Ultimately, when approached with intention and sincerity, humor and positivity don't just improve our communication skills—they enhance our lives. By embracing these principles, we have the power to transform the very fabric of our interactions, leaving lasting impressions that encourage others to likewise act positively and authentically. This, in essence, is how we communicate for the best possible outcomes, ensuring lasting connections and meaningful exchanges.

Chapter 23: Building Resilience Through Communication

In the intricate dance of human interaction, communication plays an indispensable role in fortifying our mental and emotional resilience. By using honest dialogue and active listening, we can transform potential setbacks into springboards for personal growth and emotional fortification. Resilient communication begins when we're open to feedback, even criticism, viewing it not as a threat but as a pathway to strengthen our resolve. Let's embrace the art of sharing our vulnerabilities, for in these shared moments, stronger bonds are forged and authentic connections bloom. As we navigate the labyrinth of relationships, the ability to articulate our thoughts clearly and empathetically not only builds our inner resilience but also inspires resilience in those around us. Aligning our verbal and nonverbal cues, and speaking with intention, amplifies our capacity to withstand life's challenges, allowing us to endure and thrive amidst the noise. Ultimately, when we make a conscious effort to communicate positively and effectively, we're not just nurturing our ability to cope—we're laying the groundwork for lasting personal empowerment and connection.

Coping with Criticism

When it comes to communication, criticism can feel like an unavoidable pitfall. However, instead of viewing it as a threat, approach it as an opportunity for growth. The first step in coping with criticism is to reframe how we perceive it. Often, criticism isn't personal; it's a reflection of the critic's perspective and understanding. By reframing criticism as constructive feedback, individuals can shift their mindset from defense to openness.

Emotionally, criticism can sting. Our natural impulse might be to dismiss it or react defensively. To navigate these emotions, tap into the power of emotional intelligence. Acknowledge how the criticism makes you feel and allow yourself a moment to process those emotions. This doesn't mean you need to agree with the critic, but understanding your own emotional response is key to handling it constructively.

It's important to listen actively when receiving criticism. Hearing more than just the words spoken helps you discern the underlying message. Sometimes, the way criticism is delivered overshadows its potential value. Separating the content from the tone and context can reveal insights you might otherwise miss. Remember, the essence of active listening lies in focusing on understanding rather than responding.

After you've absorbed the criticism, take time to reflect on it. Reflection allows you to assess the validity of the feedback. Ask yourself questions: Does this criticism align with other feedback I've received? Is there truth in it that I can learn from? By evaluating criticism without self-judgment, you're more likely to identify areas for improvement that might enhance your communication skills.

Constructive dialogue is an excellent way to respond to criticism. Engage the critic in a conversation that explores their perspective and clarifies the points raised. This approach not only shows you're serious about self-improvement, but it also helps foster mutual respect. A quick conversation might transform what initially felt like an attack into a stepping stone for progress.

Criticism also offers a chance to strengthen your resilience. Developing a resilient approach to criticism involves building a mental toughness that allows you to perceive feedback without letting it shake your confidence or self-esteem. It's about learning to detach your self-worth from external opinions, focusing instead on learning and growth.

In embracing criticism, we must acknowledge that not all feedback is valuable or accurate. Evaluating the source is crucial. Consider whether the critic possesses relevant knowledge or a vested interest in your improvement. Feedback from a trusted mentor or a skilled colleague is more likely to be beneficial than that from a casual acquaintance or someone with a potential bias.

Resilience is also built by reaffirming your goals and values. When your purpose is clear, criticism becomes a tool for realignment rather than a stumbling block. It can highlight areas where your actions stray from your intentions, offering a chance to recalibrate your approach and communication strategies.

Another part of coping with criticism is embracing the idea of self-compassion. Criticism doesn't define you or your abilities. Approach your imperfections with kindness rather than harsh judgment. This mindset shift encourages you to see mistakes as part of the learning process, making you more open to embracing criticism as part of your journey.

One technique for dealing with criticism is to create a mental resilience toolkit. This could include affirmation practices that reinforce your self-worth and capacities, regardless of external opinions. Regularly remind yourself of past successes and skills that bolster your self-confidence. Such practices maintain your focus on personal growth rather than short-term setbacks.

Leveraging a support network enhances your ability to handle criticism. Seek out those individuals who offer constructive insights and act as sounding boards for reality-checking feedback. With such support, you're better positioned to process criticism in a way that's productive and motivating.

While criticism may always evoke a level of discomfort, it can be one of the most powerful tools for professional and personal development. By reframing the way we receive and process criticism, we foster an environment of continuous growth and resilience. Understanding and applying these strategies ultimately leads to more effective communication and stronger relationships.

On your journey to becoming a more resilient communicator, remember that excellence often arises from the willingness to embrace discomfort and challenge. With each critique, there's potential for discovery and growth, provided we're open to its lessons. In this way, criticism isn't just something to be endured—it's a critical component of building resilience through communication.

Strengthening Personal Resilience

In today's fast-paced world, the ability to bounce back from setbacks and maintain a steady course despite adversities is an invaluable skill—one that's intimately linked with effective communication. Personal resilience taps into the heart of how we interact with others, how we perceive challenges, and how we ultimately overcome them. Building such resilience doesn't just fortify our inner strength; it enhances our communication, allowing us to connect with others more deeply and persuasively.

Resilience in communication begins with self-awareness. It's crucial to understand how our emotions and thoughts influence our reactions in trying situations. By cultivating a keen awareness of these internal processes, we lay the groundwork for resilient communication. This means recognizing our triggers and understanding how to manage them constructively. It's about pausing before reacting—choosing our words purposefully instead of letting emotions dictate our speech.

Practicing mindfulness can significantly aid in this regard. Mindfulness helps us stay present in conversations, fostering greater empathy and reducing the likelihood of misunderstandings. When our minds are present, we listen actively and respond with intention. This composed presence underpins resilience by ensuring that our communication remains clear and effective, even when tested by stress or disagreement.

Furthermore, being resilient is heavily reliant on our ability to manage stress and maintain a calm demeanor under pressure. Communication is inherently stressful, especially when stakes are high or conflicts arise. Developing techniques to manage this stress—such as deep breathing, visualization, or even temporarily stepping away from a heated exchange—enables us to communicate more effectively. These methods not only calm our minds but also ensure that our message is delivered clearly and respectfully.

Positive self-talk is another powerful tool for reinforcing personal resilience. The dialogue we have with ourselves shapes our attitudes and confidence. By replacing negative self-perceptions with affirmations and constructive feedback, we bolster our resilience. It's about reminding ourselves of our capabilities and worth, especially during conversations that may otherwise shake our confidence.

Setting realistic expectations forms another pillar of resilient communication. By understanding and accepting both our limitations and those of others, we create an environment where errors and misunderstandings are less discouraging. Instead, they become opportunities for growth and learning. This adaptability allows us to remain focused and composed, even when conversations veer off course.

Additionally, the ability to see failures as stepping stones rather than setbacks is essential for resilience. When we perceive errors as valuable learning experiences, our communication doesn't need to be flawless. It needs to be genuine and adaptable. This mindset shifts our focus from perfection to progress, making conversations more grounded and pressure-free.

Resilient communication is also about building and nurturing relationships. The support of trusted allies can serve as a buffer during challenging times. By maintaining open lines of communication with friends, family, or colleagues, we create a network of support that can uplift us when our resilience is tested. These connections remind us that we are not alone in our struggles, encouraging us to persevere.

Moreover, our resilience grows significantly when we practice empathy. By placing ourselves in others' shoes, we better understand their perspectives, creating a harmonious dialogue even amidst adversity. This empathetic approach enriches our interactions, promoting patience and understanding—a hallmark of resilient communicators.

Change is inevitable in communication, as in life, and the ability to adapt is a testament to one's resilience. Being open to new ideas, methods, and feedback ensures that our communication skills don't stagnate. Embracing change entails welcoming new communication technologies, formats, and cultural nuances, allowing us to stay relevant and effective in a continuously evolving landscape.

Resilient communication also thrives on clarity. The clearer we are in expressing our thoughts and intentions, the less room there is for misunderstanding or misinterpretation. Clarity doesn't imply rigidity; rather, it means articulating our messages with precision and openness.

This directness facilitates smoother interactions and unblocks potential barriers before they arise.

Finally, fostering resilience through communication requires consistent practice and reflection. It's important to regularly evaluate our interactions, noting what worked and what didn't, and understanding the underlying reasons. By analyzing our communication patterns, we identify areas of strength and aspects that need improvement, ensuring continuous growth in resilience.

Resilience in communication isn't built overnight; it's a lifelong journey of learning and adaptation. It's about cultivating an attitude that embraces challenges and views them as opportunities for development. By drawing on our inner strength, practicing empathy, and maintaining respectful and open dialogue, we fortify our ability to communicate effectively, even in the face of adversity.

In essence, by strengthening our personal resilience, we build a robust foundation for all our communication endeavors. This grounded foundation not only supports us individually but also enhances our capacity to connect with others genuinely and impactfully, leading to more meaningful and resilient interactions.

Chapter 24: Developing Empathy

Empathy is the invisible thread that weaves individuals into a cohesive tapestry, allowing us to truly understand and connect with one another. It's not just about recognizing the feelings of others but experiencing them as if they were our own. By developing empathy, we strengthen our ability to communicate more effectively, bridging gaps that often seem insurmountable. Empathetic communication is a dance of giving and receiving, where active listening and keen perception work in tandem to transcend words and uncover deeper meanings. Cultivating this skill requires intentional practice: setting aside our biases, genuinely engaging with others' experiences, and reflecting on these interactions to internalize diverse perspectives. As we hone this capability, we not only enrich our relationships but also empower ourselves to influence and inspire positively. Our empathetic endeavors transform ordinary exchanges into opportunities for profound understanding and mutual growth. Through this lens, communication becomes a powerful agent of change, fostering environments ripe for collaboration, trust, and authentic connection.

Understanding Others' Perspectives

In a world bustling with diverse viewpoints and experiences, developing the ability to understand others' perspectives is invaluable. It's not just a skill for effective communication; it's a profound path to enriching human interaction. When we pause to see the world through someone else's eyes, we unlock new possibilities for empathy, connection, and mutual growth. It's the bridge from isolation to understanding, turning our words into threads that weave stronger communities.

Understanding others starts with curiosity—a genuine interest in learning about the lives, thoughts, and feelings of those around us. This curiosity drives us to ask questions, listen actively, and observe keenly. It's like being an explorer in unfamiliar territory, ready to set aside preconceived notions and immerse oneself in the nuances of another's reality. Such an exploration requires an openness to learn and unlearn, to challenge one's biases and embrace new insights.

This skill is particularly crucial in communication, where assumptions can easily distort reality. Miscommunication often stems from the failure to acknowledge that each person filters their experiences through unique lenses shaped by their background, culture, emotions, and situational context. When we assume others perceive and interpret the world exactly as we do, we open the door to misunderstanding and conflict. Recognizing this discrepancy is the first step towards more meaningful conversations.

Empathy serves as the cornerstone of this understanding. It is the capacity to emotionally resonate with someone else's experience, to step into their shoes without losing our own footing. Empathy goes beyond merely acknowledging emotions; it involves recognizing their roots and acknowledging their legitimacy. When we empathize, we validate the experiences and emotions of others, making them feel seen and understood.

Imagine you're engaged in a conversation with a colleague who's expressing frustration about a project. Instead of dismissing their feelings or jumping to solutions, try to understand the factors contributing to their stress. By doing so, you're not just sympathizing;

you're empathizing. This subtle difference fortifies trust and opens the floor for constructive dialogue, fostering an environment where all voices are valued.

Developing an understanding of others' perspectives requires deliberate practice and patience. It starts with small changes in how we interact daily. Consider the importance of mindful listening, where we shift our attention fully to the speaker. Just as important is the ability to ask open-ended questions that encourage the sharing of thoughts and emotions. These questions invite deeper reflection and provide insights that closed questions can't.

A critical aspect of understanding perspectives is recognizing and managing our biases. These biases often serve as invisible barriers that prevent us from fully appreciating another's viewpoint. Whether they're shaped by upbringing, experiences, or societal influences, biases cloud our judgment and limit our openness. By bringing them into conscious awareness, we can start dismantling them and create room for genuine appreciation of diversity.

Moreover, embracing cultural humility is key—an awareness that no one culture dominates truth or morality. Every culture offers lenses that can enrich the human experience. When we communicate with people from different backgrounds, it's crucial to subdue the impulse to impose our cultural norms onto their reality. Instead, approach with a sense of curiosity and respect for varied worldviews.

Indeed, understanding other perspectives is a gateway to effective persuasion. When you truly grasp where someone is coming from, you're better equipped to frame your message in ways that resonate with them. This empathetic approach doesn't just enhance your influence; it also facilitates collaboration and innovation—qualities indispensable in today's interconnected world.

Furthermore, understanding perspectives enhances our ability to mediate conflicts. By comprehending the underlying needs and concerns of all parties, we can navigate disputes more constructively, leading to solutions that each side perceives as fair and balanced. This shift from adversarial to cooperative conflict resolution is a testament to the transformative power of empathy.

In professional settings, adopting this perspective-centric approach can lead to more harmonious workplaces. Recognizing the diverse motivations and values of team members can inspire leadership strategies that harness the strengths of individuals, fostering a more inclusive and productive environment. It's about leveraging diversity as a strategic advantage, rather than a challenge to be managed.

As you continue to hone your communication skills, remember that understanding others' perspectives isn't a destination; it's a continuous journey. It's an ever-evolving process that requires us to remain open, curious, and reflective. By cultivating this practice, you contribute to a more empathetic world, where every interaction holds the potential for deep connection and mutual respect.

Ultimately, the purpose of understanding perspectives is not merely to be more effective in communication. It's to transform our interactions from mere exchanges of information into moments of true understanding and connection. It's about creating a world where the richness of human experiences is not just acknowledged, but celebrated. Each time we make the effort to understand someone else, we take one step closer to that vision.

Cultivating Empathy Skills

Empathy is more than just understanding another's emotions; it's about seeing the world through their eyes, experiencing their joys and sorrows in tandem with them, and responding with genuine care. Yet, cultivating empathy is often deemed challenging. It requires a commitment to step beyond your own perceptions and embrace diverse human experiences. In our quest to improve communication, empathy rises as a pivotal skill, offering a bridge to deeper connections and enriched interactions.

To truly cultivate empathy, one must begin with self-awareness. This involves acknowledging your own biases and preconceptions. Our minds are filled with filters formed by life experiences, cultural backgrounds, and personal influences. Being aware of these helps in pausing before reacting, allowing space for others to express their truths. This self-awareness turns reactive tendencies into responsive interactions that prioritize understanding over judgment.

Listening is an art that forms the bedrock of empathy. It's not just about hearing words; it's absorbing the underlying emotions and intentions. Active listening positions you to reflect back on what the speaker is truly conveying. It involves engaging with the speaker, asking clarifying questions, and summarizing what's been said to ensure accuracy. This process validates the speaker's feelings and encourages open communication.

Curiosity plays a powerful role in empathy. Cultivating an open mind and a genuine interest in others' stories can transform interactions. By asking questions and expressing genuine curiosity, you not only learn more about others but also demonstrate that you value their perspective. It's about saying, "Tell me more," and meaning it, offering a genuine invitation to dialogue.

Nonverbal cues, such as body language, facial expressions, and eye contact, echo the narrative verbal communication conveys. For instance, maintaining eye contact can demonstrate attentiveness and concern, whereas nodding can signal agreement and understanding. The subtle cues speak volumes and often instill a sense of trust and empathy more robust than words alone.

Furthermore, empathy thrives on emotional regulation. Sharing others' emotions doesn't mean absorbing their emotional states passively. It's essential to manage your emotional responses consciously, ensuring you don't become overwhelmed by empathy's emotional demands. Balancing empathy with emotional intelligence allows for more constructive dialogues, where compassion doesn't morph into emotional exhaustion.

A challenge for many is the ability to empathize with perspectives starkly different from their own. This requires stepping out of one's comfort zone and willingly confronting uncomfortable truths. Engaging with diverse groups and perspectives fosters empathy. It pushes you to question assumptions and broaden your worldview, allowing empathy to germinate in the fertile ground of diversity.

Empathic communication also hinges on authenticity. This means responding naturally and sincerely to the emotions and situations shared by others. Authentic responses build a safe space for honest exchanges, where people feel heard and respected, ultimately encouraging a reciprocation of empathetic behavior.

To deepen empathy skills, reflecting on past interactions can be valuable. Consider scenarios where empathy was lacking; analyze the barriers that prevented an empathic response. Was it a misinterpretation of signals, a bias that clouded judgment, or maybe a lack of attention? Learning from these experiences turns errors into stepping stones for growth, enhancing future communication.

Incorporating perspective-taking exercises into daily routines can expand empathic abilities. For instance, engaging with literature, films, and art provides glimpses into varied human experiences, offering prepackaged vantage points different from your own. By immersing yourself in these fictional worlds, you practice understanding emotions and motives distinct from your reality.

Empathy is not a static skill; it develops through continuous practice and engagement. Making empathy a habit involves conscious effort—checking in with others about their feelings, validating their experiences, and responding with understanding. Over time, these efforts manifest as natural empathetic inclinations, paving the way for deeper, more meaningful connections.

In professional settings, empathy enhances teamwork and conflict resolution. It facilitates a collaborative environment where colleagues feel respected and heard. Empathetic leaders foster trust and loyalty, creating an atmosphere where everyone is motivated to contribute their best, knowing their voices matter.

In personal realms, empathy enriches relationships by building a solid foundation of mutual respect and understanding. It allows for emotional closeness that withstands misunderstandings and disagreements, strengthening bonds over time.

Ultimately, cultivating empathy is as much about personal growth as it is about enhancing communication. It refines our ability to connect with others on a deeper level, enabling a blend of compassion, understanding, and genuine concern. As our empathy blossoms, we pave a path toward more harmonious interactions, leading to a more connected and compassionate world.

Chapter 25: The Ethical Side of Communication

As we delve into the ethical side of communication, we must recognize the profound responsibility it carries. When we communicate, we shape not just perceptions, but realities, and this influence demands integrity and transparency. It's about understanding the powerful ripple effects our words can generate and choosing to wield this power wisely. Ethical communication blends honesty with respect, valuing truth without sacrificing the humanity of our connections. By aligning our messages with our values, we ensure that persuasion doesn't eclipse purity of intent. Imagine the transformative potential when every conversation is guided by a commitment to ethical principles, creating trust-filled dialogues that resonate with sincerity. This ethical backbone forms the foundation for authentic, meaningful exchanges, where influence isn't a manipulative force but a collaborative dance of mutual understanding.

Understanding Ethical Considerations

In the vast landscape of communication, understanding ethical considerations is paramount. It's not just about conveying a message or persuading an audience, but ensuring that our communication is anchored in integrity and respect for others. At the heart of ethical communication lies the understanding that what we say and how we say it can have profound effects on individuals and communities. This knowledge obliges us to communicate responsibly, knowing our words resonate beyond immediate interactions.

Ethical communication begins with honesty. Transparency isn't just a moral choice; it's a foundation for building trust. When we communicate honestly, we foster an environment where others feel safe enough to express themselves openly. This reciprocal honesty encourages genuine dialogues rather than transactional exchanges. It's about sharing truthfully and being forthright about our intentions, all while respecting confidentialities when they must be kept.

Respect for diverse perspectives is another critical ethical consideration. In our ever-globalizing world, we constantly encounter people from various backgrounds, each bringing unique viewpoints. Engaging effectively with these differing perspectives requires active acknowledgment and appreciation of diversity. It's not enough to merely tolerate; we must strive to understand, which involves listening deeply and valuing the insights others bring. This approach not only enhances our perspectives but also empowers others, creating a richer tapestry of communication.

Consider also the responsibility that comes with influence. In the realm of communication, influencing others is indeed a powerful tool. However, ethical communication demands that this influence is wielded with care and integrity. Manipulative practices that exploit vulnerabilities or mislead others for personal gain are not only unethical but also erode the foundational trust relationships depend upon. Instead, when influencing, the aim should be to uplift and enlighten, fostering a true sense of shared growth and understanding.

A key aspect of ethical communication involves recognizing the impact of our words on others' emotions and well-being. Words can heal or harm; they can build bridges or create divides. Ethical communicators are mindful of the emotional responses words might invoke. They are attuned to the nuances of language and the power it wields, opting always to build and never to break down. Sensitivity in communication reflects empathy, an indispensable component of ethical practices.

Privacy is an essential ethical factor, particularly in our digitally driven age. The ease with which information is shared can sometimes blur the lines of what's appropriate. Being careful with others' private information, whether shared in confidence or merely inferred, is crucial. Ethical communicators understand the importance of protecting privacy, ensuring that the boundaries of confidentiality are respected and upheld at all costs. A breach of trust in this area can have lasting effects, undermining relationships and reputations.

Furthermore, ethical communication involves a commitment to fairness and equity. It's about affording everyone an equal voice and ensuring that all parties are heard and considered. Equity in communication means giving space for marginalized voices to be amplified and respected. This could mean stepping back to allow others to step forward or using one's platform to elevate voices that might otherwise go unheard. A commitment to equity fosters inclusivity, making for a more holistic and respectful communication environment.

Accountability is another cornerstone of ethical communication. It requires owning up to one's words and actions. Mistakes are inevitable, but taking responsibility for them demonstrates character and ethical fortitude. This accountability fosters an environment where learning and improvement are encouraged. It demonstrates humility and the understanding that communicators, too, are always learning and evolving.

Balancing persuasive strategies with ethical considerations can sometimes seem daunting. It's a delicate dance between achieving communication goals and maintaining moral integrity. The key is to consistently align persuasive efforts with ethical standards. This ensures that while we aim to compel or convince, we do so with respect, honesty, and fairness. Persuasion should never be at the expense of someone else's rights or dignity; it should inspire rather than coerce.

In summary, understanding ethical considerations in communication is not just a professional obligation but a personal commitment. It's about creating a legacy of trust and understanding in every interaction, whether personal or public. As communicators, we're tasked with the responsibility of weaving ethical threads through the fabric of our dialogues, ensuring that they stand the test of time and scrutiny. By embedding ethical principles into our communications, we not only enhance our own credibility and effectiveness but also contribute more positively and meaningfully to the world around us.

Communicating with Integrity

In our quest to enhance communication skills, one might overlook the significance of integrity as a cornerstone of effective interaction. Yet, integrity in communication is undeniably foundational. It's about aligning our words, actions, and intentions to reflect honesty, respect, and authenticity. When you communicate with integrity, you create a space where trust can flourish, and genuine connections are forged.

Speaking with integrity isn't just about telling the truth. Although honesty is a critical component, it's also about transparency and consistency in what we say and do. When our actions back up our words, we send a powerful message that we can be relied upon. This trust is indispensable, not only in personal interactions but also across professional environments. It's the glue that holds relationships, teams, and organizations together.

While maintaining integrity might seem straightforward, it becomes challenging in the face of competing interests and pressures.

In a world where short-term gains often tempt us to compromise ethical standards, committing to honest communication can feel like swimming against the tide. However, the longer-term benefits of integrity—like sustained trust and respect—far outweigh any immediate advantages gained from deception or manipulation.

Consider the practice of active listening. This is where communicating with integrity comes to life. By genuinely paying attention to what others are saying without the intent to manipulate or judge, you respect the other person's perspective. This not only strengthens relationships but also cultivates an environment where open, honest dialogue can thrive, allowing for mutual understanding and growth.

Furthermore, communicating with integrity means being courageous enough to express your opinions and beliefs, even when they may be unpopular. It involves a delicate balance between asserting your views and respecting others' viewpoints. This balance is central to maintaining integrity and fostering open communication. It's about standing your ground without being combative, and open enough to embrace diversity in thought.

Let's not forget the crucial role that emotional intelligence plays in this equation. Understanding your emotions and managing them effectively allows you to communicate with integrity even in challenging situations. It supports you in responding rather than reacting, ensuring that your words are always aligned with your values and your intent is clear.

The impact of technology on communication is another realm where integrity is tested. In digital communication, where face-to-face cues are absent, maintaining integrity requires clarity and mindfulness. It's easy for messages to be misconstrued, so ensuring your digital interactions are forthright and sincere is critical. Whether you're sending an email or posting on social media, the principles of honest communication remain steadfast.

Building a culture of integrity in communication isn't just an individual endeavor; it extends to teams and organizations. Leaders who model and uphold these values inspire others to do the same, creating a ripple effect that reinforces ethical communication throughout. This collective integrity becomes a competitive advantage, fostering collaboration, innovation, and resilience.

Challenges arise most often during difficult conversations. It's here that the commitment to integrity is truly tested. Whether it's providing constructive feedback or navigating conflicts, staying true to your principles while maintaining empathy and respect can transform potential confrontations into opportunities for breakthrough understanding and growth.

Moreover, integrity in communication includes acknowledging mistakes. We're all human, and errors are part of life. When mistakes happen, owning up to them candidly and promptly can actually enhance your credibility. It shows that you are not only honest but also committed to learning and improvement.

In your journey to communicate with integrity, mindfulness plays an indispensable role. It encourages you to be present in the moment, aware of both your words and the impact they have on those around you. Practicing mindful communication helps ensure that your interactions are intentional and aligned with the ethical standards you aspire to maintain.

Ultimately, communicating with integrity builds a legacy of trust and respect. It has the power to inspire others, create meaningful relationships, and lead to profound personal and professional fulfillment. As you integrate these principles into your daily interactions, you contribute to a world where communication is not only effective but also elevates the human experience.

Conclusion

As we draw to a close on this enlightening journey, it's clear that communication is not merely a tool; it is the very essence of human connection and interaction. In every arena of life, whether personal or professional, the ability to communicate effectively holds the key to understanding, persuasion, and influence. It's a multifaceted skill that demands both awareness and practice, and this book's goal has been to equip you with practical strategies rooted in the intricacies of human psychology.

Throughout our exploration, we've ventured into the depths of perception, nonverbal cues, and the art of active listening. Each chapter has untangled the nuanced principles that drive our daily exchanges, emphasizing the significance of seeing beyond words. We've seen how perception can color conversations, often requiring us to reframe our views to truly grasp what others might be trying to convey. Nonverbal communication, too, plays an undeniable role, turning simple gestures into powerful transmitters of intent and emotion.

Active listening emerges as a cornerstone, transforming the way we engage with others. By honing our listening skills, we open doors to empathy and understanding, breaking down barriers that might otherwise hinder genuine connection. It amplifies our ability to respond rather than react, fostering an environment where meaningful dialogues can thrive.

Crafting messages with purpose and clarity becomes another thread in the tapestry of effective communication. From choosing our words wisely to structuring our messages thoughtfully, each choice we make speaks volumes. It's in these seemingly small decisions that we create impact, whether we're persuading an audience, building rapport, or leading a team. Every message is an opportunity to leave a lasting impression, one that resonates well beyond the conversation at hand.

We explored deeper into the complexities of emotional intelligence and the subtle art of maintaining composure during challenging conversations. Embracing and managing our emotions allows us to navigate intricate communications with grace and intention. In doing so, we transform potentially combative scenarios into collaborative discussions, paving the way for resolutions that are both effective and peaceful.

Communication doesn't exist in isolation; it's woven into the fabric of teamwork and leadership. The dynamics of group interactions, the art of persuasion, and the cultivation of trust and credibility are all facets where our skills are put to the test. In leadership, our words inspire and motivate, shaping visions and rallying the collective energy toward common goals.

Digital and cross-cultural communications present newer challenges and opportunities. As technology continues to evolve, so too must our strategies, allowing us to engage across platforms without losing the essence of human connection. Simultaneously, navigating cultural differences expands our perspective, enriching our capacity to communicate with empathy and respect across diverse global contexts.

Feedback and confidence form a critical part of our personal growth and development journey. Embracing feedback as a tool for learning, not as criticism to fear, empowers us to refine our skills continuously. With confidence, our voices gain strength, and we find ourselves stepping out of the shadows of self-doubt, ready to communicate effectively and with purpose.

Incorporating humor and positivity reminds us of the lighter side of communication. It creates warmth and builds bridges, allowing interactions to flow with ease and making challenging situations more manageable. Meanwhile, empathy remains the thread that connects us all, encouraging us to step into others' shoes and engage with kindness and understanding.

Looking ahead, the future of communication promises both excitement and uncertainty. As trends and innovations unfold, preparing for these changes ensures we're not just participants but pioneers in shaping how we interact and understand one another. It's an ongoing adaptation, one that calls for resilience and agility.

Above all, the ethical dimension of communication serves as a guiding principle. Communicating with integrity and transparency fosters trust and respect, values that are invaluable in every aspect of life. Our ethical compass directs our interactions, ensuring they are beneficial and constructive.

This conclusion isn't just the end of a book; it's the beginning of applying these insights to everyday life. Whether you're enhancing relationships, driving professional goals, or merely seeking to connect on a deeper level, remember that communication is your ally. It's a journey, a continuous evolution of learning and mastering the art of connecting with others.

Appendix A: Appendix

As we reach the culmination of our exploration into the psychology of communication, this appendix serves as a resource to enhance the journey you've embarked upon. The sections you've traversed have equipped you with a treasure trove of strategies and insights. Here, we'll consolidate supplementary materials and exercises to deepen your understanding and application of effective communication principles. Let's explore ways to synthesize these concepts into actionable steps that resonate in your interactions.

Additional Resources

Books and Articles Expanding your knowledge isn't confined to a single source. The listed books and articles can broaden your perspective and offer complementary views on the topics covered:

Webinars and Online Courses Engaging in interactive learning through webinars and courses can reinforce and diversify your understanding.

Podcasts
Embracing auditory learning, podcasts can offer unique insights from thought leaders and experienced communicators.

Exercises and Practice

Role-Playing Scenarios Practice real-life communication scenarios with peers, focusing on active listening, non-verbal cues, and persuasion techniques. Analyze the interactions to identify strengths and areas for improvement.

Journaling Emotions Keeping a journal of your emotional responses during conversations can help you better manage emotions and enhance emotional intelligence in communication.

Feedback Trials Initiate a routine of giving and receiving feedback with trusted partners. This practice will sharpen your skills and build resilience, contributing to personal and professional growth.

Actionable Commitments

Taking what you've learned from this book, identify specific commitments to enhance your communication skills:

Set measurable goals for the improvement of your skills, using techniques discussed in the chapters.

Regularly review and adapt communication strategies to fit different contexts and cultural environments.

Incorporate mindfulness practices to remain present and focused in every interaction.

Consider this appendix as your continuous guide, inspiring you to evolve and refine your communication skills. As you integrate these practices into your daily life, you're not only fostering better communication but also cultivating meaningful connections that can transform your personal and professional relationships.

www.ingramcontent.com/pod-product-compliance
Lightning Source LLC
Chambersburg PA
CBHW020416290526
45785CB00002B/591